Are you sure that's a saxophone?

Sarah Skinner

Are You Sure That's A Saxophone?

Introduction

It's 3 a.m. I'm whizzing down the A22 in a pickup truck with an amateur taxidermist who is fanatically trying to keep me awake with more information than I'll ever need about how to stuff a badger.

I'd called roadside assistance half an hour earlier to let them know that a) I had a flat tire, b) I didn't have a spare, and c) I was a lone female on a rather horror-story-looking stretch of pitch-black country road. In return, the operator told me that my membership had expired just the day before and they could do nothing to help. I kept the girl on the phone and described my situation a second time, labouring the point considerably with some extra detail about how *murdery* the location felt. Bless her! She pulled out all the stops and got a recovery truck to me before my racing mind had conjured up too many macabre scenarios.

I never caught the driver's name, but he was my knight in shining armour that evening for many reasons. A life-changing, career-altering stranger who knew way too much about sparrow carcasses for my liking. We talked, or rather, he talked, and I listened, sharing gruesome details about taxidermy and all the various roadkill he'd found and either stuffed or eaten over the years. I tried to look enthralled. Really I did. But as much as I nodded and said, 'cool' or 'wow' in all the right places, he soon realised his authentically dressed Civil War reenactment squirrel armies weren't to everyone's taste and gave me a wry smile.

'So, what do you do for a living?'

'I'm a musician,' I smiled back at him.

'Tell me all about it,' he said, sounding genuinely interested.

So I did. I told him about the wedding I'd just played with the dead goldfish centrepieces on every guest's table. I talked about my very first gig, where I'd earned less than an owl, and about the time I got thrown out of a hotel in the middle of the night because I *didn't* want to party like a rock star. I described a few dodgy promoters and some of the funny things audience members had said to me over the years. He reeled in horror as I revealed details of the promoter who'd warned me he'd kick my teeth in if I told anyone he'd stolen the takings, and then he laughed out loud while I regaled him with the time a host misheard me and thought I'd asked if it was OK to have sex with his wife.

Gleefully, the driver kept shouting 'more, more!' at the end of each story, so I told him about the time I played a gig in front of thousands with my foot in a bucket of ice and the time I drank coffee sambucas with Pete, the most aloof cat in Amsterdam.

As we were almost at my home, the red-bearded-taxidermist-cum-pickup-truck-driver turned to me offhandedly,

'You should write a book.'

I put the idea straight to bed and left it there for almost ten years. It ate away at me, gnawing to get out until eventually, I read yet another famous musician's biography that started with 'So, I was playing at the Frog and Bucket one day' and by the second chapter, they'd landed an opening slot for Bruce Springsteen and toured the world. It was time.

This book is for anyone who wants to know what might happen between a musician's very first gig and the *overnight success* that you read about in every single celebrity biography (or at least, all the ones I've read). This is for anyone who truly believes it takes hard work and dedication to make a comfortable living as a not-remotely-famous musician and not being talent-spotted by someone in a pub on Friday night in Wigan and suddenly becoming the Next Big Thing.

A surprising absence of talent scouts and a wealthy tawny owl

It was decided. I wanted to be a professional musician. I announced this important career decision to my mother as she sat behind me, brushing my frizzy hair under control and tying it tightly into the high bunches that always hurt my head.

'No,' said my mother, matter-of-factly, 'you will get a *'proper job'* or marry a nice young man and become a mum like me.'

These were my mother's expectations of me. She'd given up her job the moment she fell pregnant with my older brother and seemed to resent being a housewife whilst also trying to push her daughter into the same role. My mother was a sullen woman who never played with her children, never encouraged them, and I have no memory of her ever saying anything as soft as 'I love you' to anyone. Anyone. She seemed to believe that children should be seen and not heard. The idea of having a performer as a daughter seemed to repulse her to the core. I was six years old and had just had my first clarinet lesson. I mentally dug my heels in, adamant I would prove her wrong, but in the same way, realising that she was probably right and I should just do as I was told. I nagged her endlessly for music lessons, and when she eventually caved in, she made a point of slamming the door between us every time I practised. I only had to play one note, and the flimsy glass door between the dining room, where I practised, and the kitchen, where she concocted her tasteless misery "food," would come crashing shut: a not-so-gentle reminder that I was not meeting expectations.

Occasionally, I would join in with a hymn or two at church and be told to 'shush' by anyone within earshot. God didn't like that sound, and it simply wasn't an acceptable way to praise him. We were not a religious family; my mother attended church if her mother was visiting. In his teens, my brother 'found God' and became somewhat fanatical - perhaps filling the *affection hole* our mother's coldness created. My father only attended Harvest Festival. He loved looking at other people's vegetable growing efforts and then scurrying back to his allotment to congratulate himself on growing the village's longest (but stringiest) runner beans. I didn't even think I liked cooked vegetables until I turned 18 and went to college. It was salad or nothing for me before that. I often reeled at my father's ability to grow inedible vegetables and my mother's uncanny knack of taking those vegetables, boiling them until they were grey, and then exploding at us kids if she saw us pulling strings out of our teeth. If you ever have a sudden urge to eat greenish-grey mush with what feels like strands of cotton in it, drop in on my mother and tell her I sent you.

I was bored throughout most of my twenties. Nothing was hitting the spot, and I meandered from day to day in one endless sea of monotony and creative stagnation. My mother's voice echoed shrilly around my head, reminding me every day that I couldn't possibly become '*just a musician.*' I must become a '*grown-up*' with a '*proper job*' or, at the very least, a '*good little wife*'. I got '*proper job*' after '*proper job*' but could never hold anything down for long. I lasted a whole morning in one job, left at lunch and never returned to my desk. Another job lasted a week, where I was in charge of cataloguing some hideous dodgy Russian knock-off make-up. It smelled like a sea of old ladies. I was sent out on Friday lunchtime to get pizza for everyone and just went home instead. I managed to last almost a year in one job until I got fired for whistleblowing the director of I.T., who really should have known how to clear his search history. In short, *proper jobs* were never going to suit me.

In the summer of 1999, I was seriously starting to wonder about what direction my life would take. I had a suit, a desk job, and a mortgage. From the outside, everything seemed to be trundling along as it should. But, in my mind, I was always somewhere else, and in the evenings and at the weekends, I'd sneak away to find an open mic night or a jam night and remind myself how much I loved performing. The passion was starting to bubble away in me, eating away at my soul and reminding me that there was more to life than business meetings and office gossip.

At one of these open mic nights, the pub owner asked me if I'd be interested in a gig. He was looking for someone to play for 45 minutes or so at the village fete. I agreed without thinking. He was offering me a tenner, some food and the chance to perform more than just a song or two. I relished the idea.

I spent ages putting together a set list and thought long and hard about the order of the songs. I thought about opening with a well-known and upbeat cover before moving into something a little slower once I'd drawn a crowd. I pictured the audience singing along, smiling, nodding, and calling for more. I daydreamed about being picked up by a talent scout and writing a resignation letter to my boss. I imagined folding my resignation letter into a carefully crafted origami aeroplane, shooting it through his office door, and running away to live in a penthouse in Hollywood and live the glitzy lifestyle my Aunt bewilderingly complained I already had. I thought about how I would perform each song, every tiny little chord change, every lyric and what equipment I'd take with me. I daydreamed about what I'd say between songs and how I might cope with requests or encores if I ran out of songs. I'd micro-managed it to the point of obsessiveness.

What I hadn't planned for was the fact that I would be totally ignored by pretty much everyone. It hadn't even occurred to me that maybe a village fete was an unlikely stomping ground for music executives. I didn't plan for people to walk by without even acknowledging my efforts. Open mic always carried with it a certain level of camaraderie among the performers, and no matter what happened, you'd at least get a ripple of applause at the end of each song. I was unprepared for the deafening silence and oblivion the village fête crowd had unthinkingly thrust at me.

It didn't help that I'd been asked to set up right next to the stall for the local owl sanctuary. I soon learned, rather brutally and publicly, that I'm just not as cute as an owl. No one asked to have their photo taken with me. Not one person wanted to exchange cash for a pet on my head. My presence (and the fact that I was laying my soul bare for all to see) just wasn't cutting it. The owls, however, had a queue of people clutching their pound coins, all vying for a photo opportunity with Merlin the Tawny Owl and his buddies.

Thus began the illustrious start to my career as a professional musician. I had earned less than a common-or-garden tawny owl, but for ten quid, a cheese and pickle sandwich, and a packet of roast beef flavoured Monster Munch, I was hooked.

Hair flicks and misunderstandings

Musicians can get a bad reputation for being sexed up, drugged up alcoholics. I always groan when a musician is portrayed on TV as someone who a) always carries a guitar on their back everywhere and b) would sleep in their own vomit. To be fair, it does tend to be something you hear about more often than not when you read about musicians getting into trouble. I really should work on that, perhaps. But when the assumption of that role is already so ingrained in society, and you're talking to someone you just met, who is speaking in (at least) their third language, there's always a chance of a misunderstanding.

Downtown Brussels after dark is teeming with nightlife. The square is an experience I'll never forget. Surrounded by the most spectacular architecture: mediaeval turrets with uneven cobblestones on the ground, all lit up in beautiful ever-changing colours. Suitably named 'Grand Place,' it is not to be missed. The cobblestones will get to your feet after a while, nagging at you to sit down, but the Belgians are clever like that, and you have your choice of waffles and chocolate shops to perk you up and remind you to live in the moment.

I'd been booked to play a cute little café. The promoter organising it wasn't there (never a good sign). Nonetheless, Patrick, one of his regular audience members, had been tasked with ensuring the evening ran smoothly, that I had everything I needed, and letting me crash at his place for the night.

Patrick was a short guy who seemed to have nothing in his life of interest but his fringe (which he flicked and blew off his face all the time) and his bright shiny, and clearly very new wedding ring (which he also fiddled with all the time).

As I stood in front of the small café audience, Patrick was in the front row, fiddling with his wedding ring and floofing his hair all over the place. I spotted him, phone in hand all evening, texting and grinning inanely at the screen, occasionally returning his attention to me. I didn't mind, he was clearly a newlywed and in the throes of some incredibly important-at-the-time newlywed conversation: 'You stop texting first' 'No, you' ... or something.

After the gig, I sat with Patrick and a couple of others at the bar. I always love touring Belgium because whilst my French is poor and my Flemish knowledge extends to 'mind the step' (learned the hard way), I've found everyone wants to practice their English on me and buy me drinks after a gig.

Patrick's English was impeccable, but he was very shy. His hair flicking seemed very important to his persona, coyly looking sideways at me as if he was working on a Princess Diana look rather than the 1987 Rick Astley lookalike contest he was clearly grooming himself for.

I love being on tour, especially outside of the U.K. You can really get in the right headspace on tour rather than heading out for one night to play the Cat and Custard Pot pub, all the while fearing you left the gas on. Away on tour, you can relax knowing that if you have left the gas on, there's no point worrying about it. It's already too late. The thrill of new faces every night, new places, new foods, and new experiences; it's intoxicating.   Living out of a suitcase makes life simple. Sleep, make small talk (or more often genuine friendships) over breakfast, drive for a bit, kill some time drinking overpriced coffee, meet a new promoter, eat some more food, play a gig, win over an audience (hopefully), meet some more people, sleep in a new place, rinse: repeat. It is a constant cycle of learning how other people's showers and coffee machines work.

The problem with being out of the country is that you're constantly trying to stay connected on social media, keep up with promoters and accommodation for the next show and sneak in an email to your next-door neighbour (just in case they could check for funky smells or flames coming from your house). I try to pitch it very carefully, as asking for someone's Wi-Fi code the moment you enter their house is downright rude. It's a kind of, 'I'm sure you're great and all, but I want to just sit in your house and talk to other people while you stare at the back of my hand, OK?' No. Rude.

Leaving my gear locked up at the venue for the night, I grabbed my overnight bag and Patrick and I wandered down some charming little side streets. The further we got from the city centre, the less touristy it felt. It was still beautiful, but owning a car and living in a city like this would be pointless.

Not only was it incredibly hilly, but I can't imagine being able to find a parking space unless you work very strange hours and all your neighbours are nine-to-fivers. We walked for about a mile, and there was nowhere I could have parked. I was grateful for the parking spot and secure lockup for my gear overnight because I think I'd have been driving all night looking for a space otherwise.

We arrived at Patrick's house - a cute old-style mid-terrace townhouse. Patrick rented the basement and directed me through thin corridors, down some deep stairs into his kitchen. It was small and homely. The work surfaces were filled with crockery and various shiny kitchen devices; an electric carving knife, mixer, coffee maker, kettle, and much, much more. Strewn on the floor around the edges of the kitchen were boxes and boxes which, given the pile of half-written Thank-You Notes on the kitchen table, confirmed my suspicions: Patrick was a newlywed.

Patrick and I made small talk for a while. Whilst comfortable chatting and walking, Patrick's shyness overcame him to awkward new levels as we sat at the table while his hair flicking escalated to DEF-COMB 2 proportions. Realising his discomfort and wanting to check on details for the next day, I casually asked him if it would be OK to jump on his Wi-Fi.

Patrick turned a beautiful shade of scarlet. He flicked his hair rather more urgently. He fumbled with his shiny new wedding ring and twirled it furiously between his finger and thumb. This was, quite possibly, the most uncomfortable I've ever seen anyone, and I had no idea why.

Eventually, he found the words and quietly stuttered,

'She's ... she's actually away on business right now, and honestly, I...I really don't think she'd be into that.'

Patrick showed me to my room in silence. In the morning, there was breakfast on the table, a note asking me to lock the door behind me, and directions back to the venue car park.

Patrick... if by any chance you're reading this... I didn't want to jump your WIFE, and I apologise for the confusion.

Cake-flavoured beer and Hawaiian shirts

Nestled amongst endless fish and chip shops and Ye-Olde-style sweetie shops selling innumerable variations of the good old British 'sticks of rock,' we always looked forward to playing at The Bistro. Not because it was a good gig. Definitely not. Oh no. We looked forward to it because of the Bistro's remarkable chef and the mouth-wateringly long beer menu. This cute little European-style café on the South East Coast of England was on our gig list purely for the nosh.

Me? I loved the Mort Subite Kriek. A cherry-flavoured Belgian beer which melts in your mouth and is far more of a dessert than an alcoholic beverage. I always plumped for the duck with seasonal vegetables: a sumptuous rare duck breast encrusted with peppercorns and sitting on a heap of the freshest locally sourced veggies possible as if they'd been plucked straight from the earth. It was the kind of meal that goes cold while you photograph it in all its glory for your two Instagram followers. It truly was a delight, and always came with a lemon and poppyseed dip that was the icing on the whole Cake-Beer-Duck-Veggies phenomenon. Mort Subite, by the way, means Sudden Death. When you think about its non-boozy cake-like flavour in relation to its alcohol content, it is a genius name that probably caused the brewers to congratulate themselves with far too much of it. The only thing I disapprove of about Mort Subite is the walloping, relentless and frankly unexpected hangover that it causes. One shouldn't be hungover after liquid cake. It's just not right.

Playing as a jazz trio of myself, a double bass and a drummer, it always astounded me that Marc, the venue owner, without fail, forgot we couldn't fit on his stage and always ended up hastily shuffling tables around to accommodate us. It is physically impossible to fit a drum kit on a stage less than two feet deep. Even if we all stood in a straight line rather than the usual drummer-at-the-back formation. God knows we tried.

The first time we'd played there, we gave it our absolute best effort to squeeeeze onto the stage, but a quarter of the way into the first song, the kick drum had had just one too many thumps and slid off the stage. Marc saw this happen, but even on our third visit, we found ourselves explaining basic physics to him. Bless him and his waxed-to-within-an-inch-of-its-life Poirot moustache.

We set up, sound-checked and slowly munched our way through our meals, savouring every morsel. I ordered up my Mort Subite (for after the gig - I never touch a drop before or during), and Marc knew to have it on hand for the second we struck the last chord. He was good like that. He just wasn't so good at the basic science of that-won't-fit-there-ology.

The café was bright and cheery and right by the promenade. You could smell the sea air whenever anyone entered through the double doors. The wind almost never seemed to slow down, which meant the doors always took forever to swing shut again.

As we were getting ready to hit the '*stage,*' a large group of middle-aged men and women arrived and were ushered to a beautifully decorated long table that spanned the length of the cafe. It became apparent very quickly that they were there to celebrate a birthday, and it became apparent moments after that which member of the party was having their Big Day: Sheila.

Sheila was loud and brash with brassy blonde hair, far too much mascara, a leopard-print satin top and black satin pants which skimmed the floor. She screamed like a banshee being forced to ham up an impression of a banshee. Her presence soon made me realise this would be one of *those gigs*.

The louder Sheila and her cronies got, the more they asked us to turn down. Marc plodded over several times throughout the evening, looking more defeated each time.

'They want you to turn down a little more,' he'd say, and we'd turn the P.A. down even further until, eventually, it was off completely.

Marc mooched towards us and opened his mouth to ask us to turn down again.

'The PA is off. We're playing acoustic instruments. It simply isn't physically possible to play any quieter,' I explained, wondering whether this might be another drums-fitting-on-the-stage-like science lesson. He nodded and went back to the table of hyenas with their next bottle of fancy Champagne to raucous applause.

As the evening progressed, the party-goers from the table of hyenas glared at us in turn, each displaying the universal hand signal for *shut the fuck up* (flat hand lowered repeatedly). I responded with a rousing rendition of Mose Allison's great song, *Your Mind Is On Vacation,* and giggled mischievously at the line, *'You're sitting there yakkin' right in my face.'* It was the perfect choice of song for the occasion. So much so that we played it in all three sets. They didn't notice, but it raised our spirits.

The champagne flowed and the crowd got louder; we couldn't even hear each other - god knows what we sounded like by the end. I was hoarse, and it was a shitshow. Most of the other diners had wolfed down their food and left. I didn't blame them and wished I could have done the same.

At the end of the gig, I don't know why, perhaps just force of habit, I pulled out our merchandise box and plonked it on a table next to the stage. We'd cobbled together a collection of Jazz standards and made a CD. We were quite proud of it at the time, and it always gave me a real buzz if we sold a few at the end of a gig. Tonight would be a challenge, though, and I knew in my heart that we'd only make a sale if someone wanted to hear what we sounded like without the banshees and hyenas in the foreground.

The loudest of the birthday party gang stumbled towards me. I gave him my biggest smile and asked him if he wanted to buy a CD. The man stared at me as if I'd asked him a question in a foreign language.
Well, we are in a European-style Bistro, Sarah, so maybe ask him again, and speak slower.

'Would..you...like...to..buy...our...CD?' I asked, holding it up to his face for clarification.

The man was a cliché, dressed in an oversized Hawaiian shirt and cargo shorts. His putrid-smelling yellow cigarette-stained beard was an assault on most of my senses. As I stared at him, waiting to see if he'd understood what I'd said, he put his foot up on the table, displaying a raggedy brown sandal barely covering the furriest foot I'd ever seen. His talon-like toenails were as yellow as his beard, and his shorts were more revealing than I was comfortable with.

'Oh no, darling,' he replied in an extravagant and outrageously camp voice. 'I don't buy albums. I make them.' With that, he lifted his foot high in the air like a ballerina on speed, turned and minced away quickly enough not to see me picking my jaw up off the floor.

We packed away quickly, and I sat savouring my well-earned Mort Subite. Marc joined us for a beer and lamented the fact that he'd lost a lot of regular customers that evening but gestured at the yet-to-be-cleared-up table of empty champagne bottles and shrugged.

'They pay the bills,' he said. 'I'm sorry they ruined everyone's night, but at least my bank manager will be happy.'

Marc counted out some cash and wandered off to grab his diary to rebook us. As he approached us, I stood up, and the guys followed. The van was loaded, and we could easily make a quick getaway. We didn't discuss it between us, but there was something in the sea air that night, and we could all feel it. This wasn't somewhere we wanted to play again, despite the menu. It was a hard slog, and my throat was dry from singing for three hours un-amplified in a room full of blood-curdling-banshee-impersonators. It simply wasn't worth the paltry £120 between us for three hours of vocal cord sadism.

Stopping Marc in his tracks, pen and diary in hand, we headed for the door.

'Best get home before this storm hits,' I gestured out at the completely calm sea and the cloudless sky. He nodded.

Marc followed us to the door and shouted after us. 'Call me?'

I revved up the engine, and the three of us put both thumbs up and grinned back at him. Six thumbs and three forced smiles can't be taken as a contractual agreement, can it?

Sambuca and Whale circumcision

I never thought I'd find myself at midnight in a pub in Amsterdam eating a banana and bacon omelette with an extremely aloof cat named Pete. Although come to think of it, I'd driven past a sign with directions to a M*ega Snuffle Market* earlier that day, so to be propping up the bar with Pete and several coffee sambucas really didn't seem all that odd at the time.

The sambucas weren't my idea. We were the first English customers that Steve had seen in a while, and he relished the opportunity to speak English rather than pidgin Dutch. Having played the night before in Brussels and the afternoon in Antwerp, we had sped up the E19 to play at Steve's pub on the outskirts of Amsterdam at 6 p.m. Technically, that meant we'd played three shows in 24 hours and felt it was time to let our hair down a little.

The gig itself was fine. The audience was rowdy but gracious for the most part. One table of guys on a stag night was a little rowdier than I thought necessary and enjoyed heckling us all evening. At the end of the night, they pulled our poster off the wall and asked us all to sign it. I'm guessing so they could use it to remember where they'd been the previous night once their predicted hangovers wore off.

We gladly signed the poster. My comment said, 'You have been a pain in my arse all evening. Enjoy your hangover.' Surprisingly, they left seeming perfectly happy.

As the evening progressed, I sat in the pub listening to the sounds of a busy Saturday night. Picking up the occasional snippets of other people's conversations, I strained to make out the occasional English word or try my hand at translating Dutch. It seemed easy enough - just add -en to the end of any English words; I think that's how you speak Dutch, Flemish, German and all Scandinavian languages as well. Knifen-Forken-Spoonen. I may perhaps be stereotyping more than a little here, but I grew up on the Muppets and the Swedish chef, so I hope I'm forgiven.

I am convinced I overheard a couple talking about whale circumcision. Or perhaps my knowledge of Dutch wasn't quite mastered. Later in the evening, a scantily clad blonde wandered in, downed several vodkas and started singing *Sweet Caroline* at the top of her voice. Except it wasn't *Sweet Caroline*, it was 'Sweeeeeeeeeeeet Caroline, bum bum bum.' Before long, we were all joining in.

Steve was thoroughly enjoying having a few Brits to speak to. He'd emigrated to the Netherlands many years ago and was still struggling to grasp the language. I guess he didn't get the '-en' memo. As well as chattering at a million miles an hour, Steve poured drinks more freely than any of our slightly frazzled and dehydrated 3-gigs-in-24-hours bodies were ready for. Meticulously counting out three coffee beans into the sambuca I hadn't ordered, he explained how it is terribly bad luck to serve an even number of coffee beans in a flaming sambuca. He then promptly set his beard on fire.

I very quickly realised my tolerance for sambuca is not high, especially after singing for just over a quarter of the previous 24 hours. After a reasonably polite amount of trying to keep my eyes open and doing some very long blinks mid-conversation, another bandmate and I made our excuses and sauntered back to our accommodation.

We'd kindly been offered accommodation by a couple of crazy ageing Dutch hippies, Ernest and Agnes. Unfortunately, they also turned out to be chain smokers. Even more unfortunately, our beds were the three sofa beds in the main open-plan section of their apartment, and they wanted to stay up smoking and chatting. I don't smoke, and I'm not very good at being chatty when I'm tired and tipsy.

As I sat, rubbing my eyes and unsubtly yawning, I wondered if I could sneakily google the question, 'How do you throw someone out of their own living room politely?'

I woke at about 4 a.m. to hear our final bandmate returning. I heard one voice that wasn't his. It sounded like Steve, but I wasn't sure. Either way, I was too tired to figure it out and quickly drifted back out of consciousness.

I was woken at about seven by the sound of a cruise liner horn. Opening my eyes, I could see that Ernst and Agnes' apartment was high up overlooking the harbour. I wandered over to the huge windows and saw that we weren't just overlooking the harbour - we were in it! The whole apartment block was on stilts in the ocean. It was a windy day, and the trees along the harbour line were bending violently, swaying back and forth to remind us not to make any sudden movements for fear of alerting our imminent hangovers into action.

Agnes was happily humming in the kitchen and busying herself making pancakes and coffee and pouring huge glasses of orange juice. I sat watching the boats coming in and out of the harbour, content with my view of the day and thrilled at my (as yet) absence of hangover.

Eventually, as I heard the others stirring and whimpering, Agnes flew open the glass door between us and the kitchen and yelled 'breakfast' at the top of her voice. Full hangover alert kicked in, and our poor guitarist woke from his fitful sleep and made a time-sensitive dash to the bathroom. He returned several minutes later, looking greener than the water below us.

'Must have been the banana and bacon sandwiches,' he joked, desperately trying to put on a brave face for our hosts. The offer of orange juice instigated another lurch for the bathroom. Agnes became visibly frustrated not being able to practice her English for fear of being drowned out by the guttural noises emanating from the bathroom.

Steve joined us for breakfast and teased us mercilessly for being such lightweights. He'd had to close up the pub to show us home. None of us has any memory of this, but apparently, he'd looked into each of our eyes as we were leaving and made the (wise) judgment call that we would be found floating in the North Sea if he didn't help us home.

Apologising profusely to Ernst and Agnes, we made sure to place all the blame firmly on Steve. Knowing Steve well, they had no issue accepting this and invited us to return to Amsterdam in the future, but not to accept Steve's hospitality before theirs next time.

The drive back to Brussels for a few days off was quiet. We voted our guitarist to be the driver as he was the most experienced at driving in Europe. We lurched along, close to the hard shoulder, with a small currant bun and a bottle of water between us, each nibbling and sipping slowly and cautiously. Our three days off sightseeing were just a little blurred, thanks to a definite fuzzy feeling of Netherlands hospitality at its finest.

A box of kittens and a military operation

I opened the front door and there on the step, was a slightly dumpy woman with silver, shoulder-length hair with purple streaks that framed her face. The lady wore an ankle-length, brightly coloured tie-dye maxi dress and lace-up hiking boots. I had no idea who she was or why she'd knocked, but she stood there, staring momentarily before asking if she could come in. It wasn't that I didn't know her or that her appearance was more than a little unconventional that made the situation odd. It was the fact that she had a box of kittens in her arms, each mewing frantically and clambering for freedom.

'So...can I come in?' she asked as I struggled to fight the depths of my brain in case there were any memories of who she was. Nothing sprang to mind.

'I'm sorry, but...do I know you?' I asked, holding the door firmly between us, the kittens becoming more unruly by the second.

'I heard you play at birthday parties, and I'm looking for someone, ideally a duo, to play at a surprise party,' she said.

Aha... all was slowly becoming clear, although I really wasn't sure why the kittens were necessary.

'I'm sure I can help you with that,' I said, 'who is the party for?'

'It's a surprise birthday party for myself,' said the lady. 'My husband is useless, and I just don't trust that he'll get around to planning anything, so I'm taking charge.'

'This box is starting to get a little heavy. Would you mind if we came in?' asked the lady again.

'It's not really a good....'

'I'm Carol,' she said as she and her furry box of delights barged past me straight into my living room. The kittens sensed their chance and sprawled mischievously in all directions across my new carpet. Carol plonked herself onto the sofa and asked if I'd mind putting the kettle on for a cup of tea. There was something about Carol that made me think the simplest course of action was just to do as I was told, so I dutifully trotted off to the kitchen and made the tea.

'What I'm really looking for is a duo who can play a couple of sets of maybe an hour each: pop covers from the 60s to the present day, but none of that robot voice crap. Can you do that?'

We sipped our tea while I watched the miniature fluffy adventurers. Carol's 65th birthday plans were coming together nicely.

On paper, this looked like it would be a bread-and-butter, no-trouble kind of gig. I put the gig in the diary, took Carol's contact details, and we finished our tea. There was never any explanation for the kittens but as she left, she began trying to herd them up into the box. The little Steve McQueens were having none of this, and no sooner had she placed one in the box and turned around, it was mewing pitifully and working its way back out to pee on my nice new carpet again. Eventually, we gathered the kittens and I gave her a tea towel to put over the top of the box to contain the fluffy fugitives.

'Did you happen to notice how many kittens there were?' asked Carol as she left.

I had not.

The emails started the day after the kitten fiasco.

'Can you play Happy Birthday for me?' Of course. No problem.

'Would you be able to pipe some music through the speakers while you're taking a break?'

'Of course. No problem.'

Every couple of days, there was a new email from Carol asking for just a little bit more. At first, it was harmless. Of course, we'd play Happy Birthday for her. Of course, we could play 'Lady In Red'. Ensure there are a few Duran Duran tracks on the recorded playlist? Sure thing.

As time progressed, I realised just how much of my time was being taken up by Carol. I didn't mind, she was a nice lady - if a little eccentric - but her emails started arriving at least once a day.

By the time we reached two days before the gig, Carol was in full military mode. She had designed an Excel spreadsheet with all the songs (both recorded and performed) she wanted to hear on her birthday. She had placed a start and end time next to each song, with suggestions of what she wanted us to say between songs, how long our break was to be and what we were allowed to do during the break. (No fraternising with the local celebrity she'd invited, no drinking, no deviation from the playlist.) Carol had also listed off all the finger foods that would be available on the night and what possible allergens were in each of them. We were permitted to take some of the food, but we were not to 'take the piss.'

I was starting to feel like a contractor hired to replace a kitchen sink, but upon agreeing to my price and terms, I was expected to build a seven-storey mansion, complete with a swimming pool, tennis courts and a fully stocked library for the same fee.

Needless to say, we were very much on edge when we arrived to set up at Carol's birthday party. We'd not learned most of the songs she'd requested. We simply didn't have time, and honestly, they were such bizarre songs that we didn't feel working on them would be a good use of our time. We'd never need them again. So, we arrived both prepared and unprepared. Prepared for an evening of not meeting expectations and unprepared to meet Carol's to-the-second set list expectations.

We needn't have worried. When we arrived, Carol's husband, Dave, pulled us aside. Dave was a tall and wiry man with a kind smile and a definite sparkle of cheekiness in his eyes. I liked him immediately.

'She's a bit tanked up,' he said, in a very posh Surrey accent that suited his corduroy trousers, cravat and waxed jacket.

'I know how much effort you've put into meeting her requirements, and I know she can be difficult, but I don't think you need to worry. Someone seems to have flipped her silly switch.'

I giggled. *'Flipped her silly switch'* was a phrase I would add to my vocabulary! At that very moment, a deafeningly loud guffaw came from the other side of the room. There was Carol, her purple and grey hair backcombed and teased to within an inch of its life. Wearing a '*posh frock*' worthy of Margo from The Good Life's wardrobe and looking like it had come from a rather fancy 70s-themed charity shop, Carol was, despite the lack of guests yet, already the life and soul of the party.

The gig was fantastic. I don't know whether it exceeded expectations because I'd been so wound up about it or whether it was genuinely fantastic. Either way, everyone in that room was thrilled at our song choices, our between-song banter and the recorded music we'd managed to find from Carol's list.

The Monday after her birthday, Carol emailed me to thank me for a great evening and to apologise for 'being such a numpty' about the setlist.

I never did find any extra kittens. Carol truly was not only as mad as a box of kittens but an unknown number of boxed kittens.

Ant colonies and dictionary definitions

I swear, sometimes, when you take on a new role, it would be a good idea to be given a job description, a dictionary definition, or at least some idea of what the role entails. Take, for example, *'promoter'*. There are plenty of good ones out there, but they don't make good stories, so here, for those who may not know what this prestigious role encompasses, are some Oxford English Dictionary definitions:

Promoter: A person or company that organises or provides money for an artistic performance or a sports event.

Promote: give publicity to (a product, organisation, or venture) so as to increase sales or public awareness.

Here is the Oxford English Dictionary definition of *'performer'* to help clarify the situation further and perhaps to launch a deliberate poke in the eye in the general direction of shitty promoters;

A person who performs for an audience in a show, concert, etc.

I'm all for a band helping promote a show, don't get me wrong, but if the promoter does *nothing* and then blames the band, I take exception. I wonder sometimes if I could get away with getting up on stage, muddling through half a song, and then insisting that the promoter take over the job because I've done my best. Absurd, right? But exactly the same situation, just in reverse.

Now that we've cleared that up, I can tell you about when I was booked to play at a blues club in the North of England with a four-piece band. The 'promoter' for the venue didn't seem to know his arse from his elbow when it came to his role, so about three weeks before the gig, he emailed our agent to say he'd have to cancel it because no tickets had been sold and that he was on holiday for another couple of weeks in Spain.

The band had done well at this particular venue (under new management = red flag) before, so I spoke to the booking agent to make a few delicate enquiries about the marketing done to date by the venue. We'd spent weeks trying to get the ticket link information so we could share it on our social media, whilst the *'promoter*'s' (I'm sorry, I can't bring myself not to put it in air quotes) social media was littered with endless photographs of his lobster-red pot belly perched on a sun bed somewhere in Spain. From what I can understand, the *'promoter'* hadn't put tickets on sale, hadn't put any posters up, or mentioned the gig anywhere searchable on the internet. Finding any evidence of the event was impossible, even if you knew what you were looking for. Mystery solved. Our dear booking agent told him that perhaps once he started advertising and perhaps even - dare he suggest - put tickets on sale, maybe, just maybe, the event might be slightly more successful.

Surprisingly, this was not met well, and according to our agent, the promoter had a 'splendid hissy fit,' said he was on holiday, our gig was off, and it was 'tough titties.' The problem was that we had shows in that area the night before and the night after, so this left us with two weeks to get a replacement gig or shell out for accommodation and have a day of sitting around.

Unfortunately, superb though our agent was, no date was forthcoming in those two weeks, so we decided to throw a tent in the back of the van and slog our way up the M6 to the first of four gigs in the North.

On arriving at our chosen campsite (which had looked lovely on the website), we were greeted by a friendly young woman whose blonde hair was tied back in a gorgeously messy plait that floated down her back. She had a slightly bedraggled look as if she'd been chasing sheep around a field for most of her life. The sheep lady directed us down to the lower two fields and told us we could pitch anywhere.

As we pulled the van into the first field, we saw only one other pitch in use. A young child's toys were strewn around the open tent, and various plates of half-eaten food sat on the picnic table. Two pairs of hiking poles leaned up against the open boot of the car parked next to the tent. I yelled hello to see if we could meet our new neighbours, but there was an eerie silence.

Walking over to the picnic table, I noticed that the half-eaten plates of food on the picnic bench had been there a while. Mould was starting to grow on the bread, and some little bits of chopped-up ham and cheese had a rather impressive colony of ants on them. The whole scene made me uncomfortable. It was as if time had just stood still, and our potential new neighbours had simply vanished into thin air. It felt really sinister, and a shiver ran involuntarily down my spine. I felt unsafe but mentally slapped myself for being so spooked.

We decided to wander back up to the main building to see if we could find the bedraggled sheep-lady again in the hope that she could shed some light on our missing neighbours. The young woman was standing in the office behind the information desk, eating a mint chocolate *Cornetto* from the ice cream cabinet next to her. I spoke to her about the situation in *'Field 2'*. She looked absentmindedly into the distance,

'Yes, I thought that was weird too,' as she flicked her hair out of her ice cream. 'They said they were going for a walk in the hills a couple of days ago, and I don't think we've seen them since,' she said, seemingly still unflustered.

'Do you think you should perhaps call the Police?' I asked. The sheep-lady seemed more determined to finish her ice cream than to investigate a missing family.

'Oh...,' she said distractedly, still more concerned about her ice cream melting. 'Yes, I'll get right on that.' And with that, she picked up the old-fashioned 80s rotary phone, put her pencil into the number 9 and began to make the call without any hint of concern or urgency.

This wasn't a place we wanted to stay at any longer. It felt like we had just driven into scene one of a dreadfully cheesy horror movie where the unsuspecting group of musicians set up camp in a murder zone, despite being given plenty of warnings. No. This was not where we would be spending the night.

Leaping back into the van and letting the sheep lady know, 'We'll be off now,' we sped down the single-track road back to the dual-carriageway that led back to more populated areas. Hastily googling for accommodation, we found a gorgeous 4-star hotel with a Groupon that night. Comfortable beds, complimentary breakfasts, almost as cheap as the campsite had been and, most importantly, (as far as we knew) not a serial killer hangout. We all slept very soundly that night.

I checked the news in that area for the following few weeks, convinced I would hear of some kind of missing persons tragedy in the hills. I heard nothing. Maybe they were just on holiday, and no one fancied tidying up. Maybe their bodies were disposed of Dexter-style, or maybe our over-active imaginations had gotten the better of us.

Divas and carpets

I have a love-hate relationship with playing at outdoor festivals. I love the audiences and their reactions and the feeling of being on a big stage. I don't love the unpredictable weather and the possibility that the band going on after you have egos the size of small planets.

I was minding my own business sitting backstage at a festival in the 'green room' tent, scrolling mindlessly through social media, sprawled on a gigantic orange velvet sofa. We were due on stage shortly, and I was killing time. There's always so much time-killing before a show, and festivals are some of the worst waits because everything is such a rush the moment you are needed. Still, you're expected to be on hand for hours just in case the band before you pull out or any other reason the festival organisers can come up with. I'd been sitting for about four hours and had read the internet. All of it. It was mind-numbing. Worse still, I knew the festival wasn't running on time. There would be much more sitting to do before I was given a 30-second warning to spring into action. How was I supposed to time my pee break?

As I sat, the vocalist from the band booked to play after us sauntered in. I realised quickly that he hadn't spotted I was there, and before I could announce my presence, his behaviour indicated to me that I should just keep very quiet and hope he didn't spot me.

Backcombing his hair like an early 80s pop star in the huge great full-length mirror, the guy started to talk to himself.

'You've got this,' he said. 'You are a fucking god,' he continued, and then in the best true cockney accent, 'You, my son, are gonna fuckin' nail this.' He stopped talking briefly to fluff up his hair and begin applying black eyeliner. All the time, I was trying to remain unnoticed whilst also trying not to giggle. It wasn't from some sordid desire to mock the guy. It was more from the fact that we'd met briefly at a previous festival when he'd called a friend of mine an egotistical diva. He clearly knew how to spot one.

Dave, the festival organiser, wandered in looking for me. Sheepishly making my presence known and knowing how utterly embarrassed this could make the poor diva, I decided it would be best to pretend I'd just woken up from a nap and hadn't heard a thing.

He knew I had from the colour that flushed into his cheeks. Still, I had no time to think about his ego. I had a gig to play. It went well, all things considered. The sound man gave us and the audience a lengthy display of his superb ability to create howling feedback whilst we gave our best display of pretending the noise wasn't bothering us. It was a real team effort.

We started moving our equipment off the stage at the end of our set. Ego-guy leapt on the stage and shoved me out of the way. Like, elbow-in-ribcage deliberate shoving. Clearly, this was an attempt to put me in my place, and I shoved back. I'm a woman in a very male-dominated career, and I've been pushed around (physically and emotionally) one too many times. I was learning to stand my ground. He seemed surprised and decided to start barging into the other members of my group as well as a couple of the stagehands. All this was happening in front of the audience he was about to try and win over.

The rest of his band seemed to harbour the same deep loathing of humanity and carried their equipment onto the stage, despite being asked repeatedly by the stagehands to hang fire until it was clear of our stuff. I know from experience how many instruments, cables and various peripherals can be lost at quick changeovers at venues. I also respected the stagehands' attempts to quell this band's enthusiasm to bully us off the stage. *Every single* stagehand and *every single* member of my band asked the guys to be patient. We'd specifically told them that *every single thing* on the stage belonged to us. They all totally ignored us and loaded their equipment onto the stage as if they were deaf. In response, we all decided that this might be a lesson in self-restraint and respect and stood at the side of the stage, watching them meticulously get everything exactly how they wanted.

The drummer was making tiny adjustments to his kit. The vocalist was floofing his hair again and tying scarves to the mic stand a la Steven Tyler. The guitarist and bassist were turning their amps up far beyond what was reasonable for the size of the audience. They were ready.

The vocalist approached the mic, opened his mouth to speak, and the sound engineer muted him. One of the stagehands climbed back onto the stage and pointed at the floor.

'We're not quite ready for you yet. That's the other band's rug, and they have another gig to get to straight away, so you'll need to move all your stuff so I can grab it.'
Our drummer turned to me, grinning,

'I feel smug. Do I look smug?'
Out of morbid curiosity, I checked the band's Facebook page the next day: we were divas, the stagehands were unprofessional, and the festival was crap. They quit within the year.

Silk ties and prophylactic microphone covers

'I'm sorry, but we don't accept garments with politicians printed on them as payment. I'm sure you understand.'

We were setting up for a double-header (equal billing to both bands) with an elderly guy who wanted to be treated like a rock star. The venue's soundman made it abundantly clear that he didn't know how to plug anything in, so our guitarist offered to take over. The soundman beamed, nodded, went to the bar, and we never saw him again anywhere near the stage all night.

Maurice, the self-proclaimed rock star, was a scruffy hippy-looking guy. He looked and smelt like he had spent his life living in a campervan, playing for tips in bars. Judging by how he was walking, I guessed he was being paid in beer that night.

Maurice confided in us that he suffered from stage fright and asked if we would mind going on first so that he could quickly recce the town and find something that would 'calm his nerves.' We told him we thought there was nothing to worry about. It was a pretty small venue; even if it were full, there'd probably only be about 80 people in it. Judging by the noise in the bar already, it was unlikely any of them were planning on paying attention anyway.

Nonetheless, Maurice left us to do our sound check, and he disappeared off shouting,

'I'm gonna get high, man.'

We sat backstage sipping tea and feeling very rock and roll before the venue owner came and offered free drinks. None of us drink when we're working. Not a drop. It makes me sing sharp, and it makes another band member sing flat, so if we're harmonising, it truly sucks. It also makes us think we're pulling off good solos when we're not.

'Oh, don't be so boring, you can have one,' he said, cajoling our drummer with his elbow.

'I don't drink when I'm working,' came back our standard response.

'Yeah, but you're not working, are you... you're playing,' said the venue owner.

I had a feeling it would feel more like work than usual.

Just as we were about to start, a rather large Eton-public-school-looking man approached me. He introduced himself as Johnathon Flinkenthrop (or something equally posh sounding) and then stared at me as if I should know who he was. I didn't, which seemed to annoy him rather. He had the most ridiculously plummy-affected voice. I found it hard not to giggle. He was cliché number two of the evening, after Maurice.

There was a cover charge for the evening. I forget what it was - mostly because of Mr Flinkenthrop's next move. Reaching into his *man bag*, he pulled out four crisp, new, brightly coloured silk ties. Each of them had the first British Prime Minister, Sir Robert Walpole, on them. He placed them on the table before him and placed a pirated CD of another band's music on top of them. Gesturing to them, Johnathon Flinkenthrop (whoever he was) let me know that they were a gift from him instead of the cover charge.

Clearly absolutely loaded with both money and alcohol, he didn't see this as remotely odd and was horrified when I insisted that neither our landlords nor we took payment in silk ties and bootleg CDs. Reaching into his wallet, he pulled out one of a huge wodge of one-hundred-pound notes and asked me for change. I told him I didn't have it (half hoping he might just donate it). Mr Flinkenthrop grabbed it back from me, gesturing with an imploring look back to the silk ties. I wandered off and left the pub manager to deal with it.

We played our set. It was fine. We all kind of enjoyed it and played mostly to each other, nodding in appreciation of decent solos or particularly cool drum fills. One couple was paying total and utter attention to us. Elbows on the table before them, gazing, nodding, smiling. These were our people.

Old Mister Silk Ties must have eventually sorted out his payment method as he sat at a table near the front and began heckling us immediately.

In the middle of a chorus, Flinkenthrop yelled,

'WHERE ARE YOU FROM?' He then repeated himself louder and louder and louder until we stopped the song.

'ENGLAND,' I shouted, and we started up again. The crowd laughed

'WHERE IN ENGLAND?'

We had the crowd on our side, so our drummer shouted,

'Oh, I dunno... LONDON?'

More giggles from the audience, especially the two in the front row that we'd connected with earlier.

'WHERE IN LONDON?'

I'd had enough, and with my mouth close in on the mic, I called out,

'How about we say... 123, LONDON ROAD, LONDON.'

The crowd roared with laughter. They could see that we'd turned the situation around and were clearly just making stuff up to take the piss. Mr Silk-Ties-fancy-pants was silenced, and we continued the gig without any more hitches until...

Maurice returned from his high-searching trip, and by the smell of him, and the way he was walking, it was clear he'd been successful.

Stumbling to the front of the room, Maurice dragged a stool onto the stage and started complaining that we hadn't vacated it quickly enough. We were still in the middle of what we had planned to be our penultimate song. Plugging his guitar in, he stomped across the stage and started playing a completely different song to us. It wasn't the smoothest transition between bands. He noodled around on his guitar for a while and then stopped, waiting for applause. No one was quite sure what was happening.

Maurice grabbed my mic stand and started setting it up for his seated height. I think I was pretty respectful, all things considered. I don't share mics with anyone, especially not someone whose breath smelt like a hundred decaying skunks. He grew instantly aggressive and pulled a condom out of his wallet and started trying to pull it on over my mic and calling me a 'hygiene freak.'

I called him a dick, suggested what he could do with his condom, unplugged my mic, and went and sat with the couple who'd lit up the room for us all evening. We had a wonderful chat, and I formed a really solid friendship with them. They told me that if I were ever in the area again, I would be welcome to stay with them. Some people just get it. They handed over a scrap of paper with their address and phone number on it.

To this day, every Christmas, I still send them a card. On the back of it, the sender's address reads *123 London Road, London.*

A vindictive wasp and a new stage look

The little shit just flew straight out of a flower and fucked up my day for no reason. There I was, out for a minding-my-own-business walk on the morning of a gig, and a wasp with an Anti-Social Behaviour Order decided to use my ankle for its morning target practice. Today was going to be a challenge.

I was listed with an agency and always readily available in my local area for last-minute dep gigs (where I step in for a covers band at short notice if they have a band member unavailable - like a supply teacher, but with a band instead of a classroom).

These gigs were great *chops* builders, and I always enjoyed rising to the challenge. Sometimes they're for wedding bands, other times for tribute bands, but if I'm available, I'd happily step in. Usually, if the band were organised enough, I'd get a set list in advance; otherwise, it'd be the occasional *baptism of fire* and hope the audience doesn't notice.

On one such occasion, I got a call that a popular local tribute band needed me for a big outdoor festival. This was to be an 8-piece 80s band, and I was to be part of a horn section. It was something I was most definitely looking forward to.

I called the agency and let them know about the delinquent wasp. I told them that it might be an idea if they could find anyone else, but I'd find a way to get through it if they couldn't. I'd committed to it and didn't want to let them down. The girl on the other end of the phone was very sympathetic but said there wasn't time to find anyone else, and they'd really appreciate me pulling out all the stops and doing the gig, even if I had to sit down to perform.

My ankle decided to react spectacularly to the sting, and by the time I was due to leave for the gig, my entire foot looked like a pink rubber glove that had been blown up to the point of almost exploding. There was no way I could drive, so I managed to grab a lift with a friend and off we went.

Dosed up on anti-histamines, I napped all the way. On arrival, I could see there were around 3,000 people in the audience. An ABBA tribute band were on stage. Miming their hearts out to a backing track and each member looking maybe 40 years older than they should. It truly was cringe-worthy. We were on next.

It was almost impossible to walk on my ankle. It was so swollen I couldn't get my shoe on it and decided to hop over to the St. John's Ambulance tent and show them the damage. A young medic took pity on me and went off searching for a bucket of ice.

So... I went ahead and played a gig in front of 3,000 people with one foot in a bucket of ice and dosed up on antihistamines. It was a whole new stage look for me... and one I wasn't entirely sure about.

I was glad I wore a hat that day. Seconds before hopping on stage, I discovered that all but one of the other band members were also stand-ins. The only original member was the trumpet player, and from his collection of scraps of paper clipped firmly to a music stand, he looked more unprepared than all of us.

The first song was brass-heavy, allowing the sound engineer to demonstrate he was wholly and unflinchingly unqualified for the job. By the end of the song, he'd just about found the unmute button for the sax and trumpet mics. After this, we soon discovered that the drummer occasionally added half a bar. I'm unsure if this was intentional to keep us even more on our toes or if he genuinely couldn't count. Either way, it added to the challenge.

I pulled my hat down further over my face and put my shades on. This was a real car crash of a gig.

Somehow, two excruciating hours later, it was all over. The audience had danced happily, utterly oblivious to the maelstrom that had been happening on stage. I hopped down the steps, and the trumpet player kindly carried my bucket of now-luke-warm water. He complimented me on such a unique stage look, winked, and disappeared to the beer tent.

I never heard from any of the other deps again from that gig. I'd been the only female in the band that day, and it felt like quite a *boys club,* so I was unsurprised. A week after the gig, I got a call from the agency, asking me if there'd been any issues that night and whether I was happy with the booking. I mentioned it had been extremely tricky because no one seemed to have a clue what the plan was all afternoon but that the audience had been very happy, and that's what counts.

Bill, the agency manager, had a stern and very gruff deep voice. He clearly hadn't got the message about my wasp attack. He told me there had been several complaints about my stage presence not being as expected and that I should perhaps take a long hard look at this. If I was going to deputise in tribute bands, I needed to fit in and not try to come up with, as he put it, 'some fancy-ass-quirky attempt at standing out.' He never sent any further work my way.

No words

My jazz partner and I had been booked to play in a pub in Yorkshire for a couple of hours on a Sunday afternoon. The landlord, Bill, had told me that this was the prime spot for a 'nice bit of jazz' and asked if we could make sure that we played a set that would appeal to his usual crowd of 'people taking their mums out for Sunday roast.' We could do that, no problem. We agreed on a fee and put it in the diary.

When we arrived, we knew instantly that something wasn't right. The room had an ominous air about the place and a true sense of sadness. We quickly noticed that everyone, including the landlord, was dressed smartly and in black. All the signs pointed to this being a wake, and I pulled the landlord to one side, asking if he was sure he wanted music that day. We were OK to step aside if the situation required. Several people were openly weeping, and it just didn't seem like music - especially the upbeat jazzy set we'd prepared - would be appropriate.

Bill half smiled at me over his wide-rimmed glasses. His face wore a heaviness that seemed to age him. The yellowing of his moustache edges, the deep lines across his face and the bloodshot eyes all told a tale. Bill was tired: either of life or perhaps just of today. It was hard to tell.

'I think some music would help,' he said, moving a table or two out of the way so we could set up.

'But keep it light.' He stared earnestly at me until I nodded. Even with my limited understanding of the situation, I could see this was no time for us to launch into 'Happy Days Are Here Again.'

Tiptoeing through songs on the fly at what is obviously a very sombre event called for some extreme last-minute tenacity. Changing lyrics seconds before they come out of your mouth and choosing to scrub the likes of 'It Could Happen To You,' 'There Will Never Be Another You,' and 'In A Sentimental Mood' from the set list is hard on the brain cells. We pulled out our book of Jazz Standards and leafed through it, picking out songs on the fly that we might get away with.

No one paid any attention. I had no problem with this and wanted to get our involvement in this harrowing situation over as soon as possible. I felt like an intruder. I didn't feel unwelcome, but I felt somewhat like someone who had turned up for jury duty in a black and yellow striped bumblebee costume. Like someone who keeps telling jokes despite no one laughing. Our presence was incongruous, and for the first time in my career on stage, I felt like a fish out of water. It's one of the few times ever that I didn't enjoy being on stage, and I found myself wrestling with self-doubt and getting wrapped up in my own thoughts, trying not to focus on the situation in front of me.

When our set was over, I sat at the bar to settle up with the landlord while my partner packed away our gear. I was hoping to get away as quickly as possible.

Bill hopped out the back to grab some money for us and, bless him, a plate of sandwiches for the road, and as he did, a young woman sidled up to me. Her mascara had run down her face, and her eyes looked puffy and swollen. Clearly, the event had something to do with someone very close to her. As she got right next to me, she threw both arms around me and just sobbed. It was clear that she needed this, and I hugged her back and gave it as long as she needed before she pulled away and wiped her face.

'Thank you so much for playing at my son's wake,' she said.

'He was only six months old, but he always smiled when there was music on the radio.'

There are just no words. My eyes said everything they needed to. I knew that if I spoke, I'd burst into tears. I think she knew that too. My *bad day at work* paled into insignificance compared to her pain, and we hugged for just a little longer before she returned to her family, and I returned to the van to remind myself to be grateful for every last second.

Fish, chips and Beefcakes

Johnny was a guy who knew everything there was to know about Fish and Chips. Critics, foodies, and locals revered his restaurant in the North of England. Johnny knew Fish and Chips. There was no doubt. The restaurant, unassumingly named 'Johnny's', was a one-of-a-kind spot: a seemingly frill-less greasy spoon, but with incongruously fancy silverware, white linen tablecloths and waiters dressed in monogrammed tuxedos.

Not content with serving up exactly what his restaurant was winning awards for, Johnny was keen to push the corners of his Chip Empire and decided on a whim one day to install a stage and start booking bands. Johnny had a dream of a ticketed dinner-and-a-concert-type evening and figured some jazz might be the way to get the ball rolling. Cue this guinea pig and her four-piece jazz band.

As we arrived, Johnny came out of the kitchen to greet us. He was a huge guy who smelled of chip fat (unsurprisingly), with a bald head and eyes that didn't seem big enough for his vast expansive sweaty face. The eyes just sort of sat there, dangling from his Dennis Healey eyebrows like little Newton's Cradle balls darting left to right nervously.

I reached out to shake his hand and instantly regretted it. I would spend the next hour or so returning to the bathrooms to wash my hands repeatedly in a vain attempt to stop my now greasy little fingers from ending any chance of soloing tonight.

Johnny opened his mouth to speak. He caught me off-guard. It wasn't any standard pleasantry that you might expect,
'You won't be able to play at your normal volume tonight.'

How bizarre! How does he know what our normal volume is? Does he think that we went through all the volume options for tonight's gig and chose *too loud* as the one we'd settle on?

Without further explanation, he pointed towards the makeshift used-pallet stage, muttered, 'That's you,' and shuffled back to the kitchen. I did wonder how differently the evening would have gone if I'd responded with, 'You won't be able to make your normal menu tonight,' but the opportunity was lost long before I had the chance to speak.

We set up, sound-checked, and seemingly we weren't *too loud* because, at one point, Johnny came out of the kitchen, raised an approving greasy thumb, and disappeared again.

As people arrived, I enjoyed greeting them at the door. I like to meet new people, and if they're paying to see me, then I should at least make an effort to mix with them and not just entertain them. I love shaking hands with someone who has no idea who I am or why I just thanked them for coming, only to do my damndest to win them over for the next couple of hours. I doubt famous artists hang around in the foyer before the show at the venue they're to be playing but screw them: I am decidedly un-famous and doing what I damn well please, thank you very much.

As one group arrived, I overheard them tell Johnny they didn't have tickets. They didn't want to see the band and they didn't want to pay for the music: they just wanted a meal. It seemed Johnny believed he knew as much about gig promotion as he did about chips, so he decided that was just fine. He parked the group just to the right of us and level with the stage. After all, they'd said they didn't want to *see* the band, not that they didn't want to *hear* it.

The moment we started playing, the group began shouting over the top of us. I gave them all my best Paddington-like stares, but it wasn't working. They just got louder and louder. At one point, I turned to look at them, and they were all mouthing '*fuck you*' at me. Charming!

We had a truly emotional song in our set at the time - a lullaby-like ballad written by a couple of us. Whenever we got the chance to play it in front of a listening audience, it was always a very special part of the gig. It truly connected with people, and we've seen many a tear shed whilst playing it. I like holding the audience's emotions in my hands and taking them on a rollercoaster. Not tonight, apparently, because at this point, the table next to me decided to start singing some football chant at the top of their voices. My patience was running as low as my self-esteem.

Just when I was about to insert my sax into the loudest member of the group, a man on the other side of the room caught my eye. A tall man: a big, strong-looking beefcake of a man. Perhaps a police officer, based on his confident strut. The man got up from his table and wove between every other table, ensuring he got every audience member's attention. Round and round he walked, smiling at every single table as he went. Slowly...slowly, until he reached the table on my right. Leaning over the table, his smile disappeared.

'SHUT THE FUCK UP.'

A short, tattooed man with a mop of salt-and-pepper hair made half an attempt to square up to him, but as he did, a wonderful thing happened. Every single paying audience member in the room rose to their feet and started cheering. The applause was positively deafening. In no uncertain terms, this remarkable man had said what I'd been trying politely to indicate to this table all evening. *Beefcake* towered over him, and the tattooed man sat back down, the colour of his face matching the colour of his Manchester United football shirt.

As the applause died down and *Beefcake* returned to his seat, I profusely thanked him and promised him a beer after the show, to which most of the audience chimed in and offered him one too. It was a marvellous bonding moment, and I hope that poor angel didn't accept too many of those beers for the sake of his liver.

The noisy table observed all of this in total silence. We continued with the gig, and during the next song, they all shuffled out, leaving their meals half-eaten. Johnny mentioned afterwards that they'd asked him to apologise to us on their behalf, but I think it was more of a gesture on his part and a recognition that perhaps he'd made a mistake letting them in.

At the end of the evening, Johnny shook my hand greasily again and let us know he thought our show had been a great success. We weren't, in fact, *'too loud'* but actually *'really rather good'* after all. He pulled out his diary to discuss a rebooking. I told him I'd pop out to the van and grab my diary.

I hope he's not still waiting for me. It's been twelve years now.

Sofa beds and dog poop

The sign on my host's bedroom door said;

NO ENTRY. STRICTLY NO ENTRY. I MEAN IT. DO NOT COME IN EVEN IF THERE IS AN EMERGENCY. IN FACT, DO NOT DISTURB ME UNLESS THE HOUSE IS BURNING DOWN AND EVEN THEN, PLEASE CONSIDER IF IT'S SERIOUS ENOUGH TO DISTURB ME.

House concerts are always pretty hit-and-miss. They can be amazing. They can be terrible. Almost nothing in your communications with the host before the event gives you any indication of which way things are going to go. The good thing about house concerts is a guaranteed bed for the night, an attentive audience and the chance to make some new friends. Usually, I love them.

Tonight's house concert had been at a small mid-terrace townhouse in the centre of York. I'd already been giggling to myself all day whilst observing town names en route - my favourite being a village called Nether Poppleton just before I arrived at the gig. I was in high spirits when I arrived to meet my hosts, John and Kate and their overly energetic British Bulldog puppy, Diesel.

Diesel leapt through the front door as I stood on the mat and head-butted me affectionately in the kneecaps. Not content with the display of affection achieved so far, Diesel jumped up and down like a stray rubber ball on the tarmac of a kids' playground. Licking and gnawing at my hands as John beckoned me indoors, I could already tell Diesel was going to be the featured performer of the evening.

Typically when I arrive at a house concert host, they show me around, point out the bathroom, my bedroom and other important locations (such as the fridge) and then we sit down for a good chitchat before I set up and they busy themselves putting out chairs and making snacks. Not tonight. Almost as soon as I'd finished the pre-approval-Diesel-licking fest, John told me he had a deadline to meet for work and that he'd be off upstairs working until the gig started. He trotted off, leaving me with Kate.

All of my conversations about the gig so far had been with John, so I relished the opportunity to get to know Kate. Kate was extremely tall and thin, with little pixie ears that peeked out from her poker-straight waist-length hair. Dressed from head to toe in purple linen with a paisley print and bare feet, she gave the impression of someone who wanted everyone to know she was a free spirit. Either that or she was just supremely cool and definitely someone I was looking forward to connecting with.

Kate told me John's work was very important and very demanding of his time. I asked several times what he does for a living, but each time I asked, Kate evaded the question and talked about the various signs he puts on the bedroom door to make sure she stays out. She spoke about *Category Five* signs which said something like 'I'm working, but if you fancied bringing me a cup of tea, I'd be ok with that,' right up to '*Category One*' signs: 'Keep the fuck out of here. Your life depends on it.' Kate flashed me a grin as she described her partner's quirks and shrugged, 'He's so important, you know.'

Guests began to arrive, and Diesel spiralled into a full-blown lick-a-thon, inspecting everyone, nudging them and head-butting them, demanding attention from each guest until the next arrived.

John emerged from his def-com two work session upstairs, and I gladly got on with entertaining the eclectic crowd of people who were happy to come out on a Tuesday night to see a girl perform a few songs. There were probably about 20 bodies squeezed into that tiny little living room, and it got warmer as the evening went on. A few faces, in particular, caught my eye: a stern-looking guy dressed in black with a trilby hat in the front row, a younger man with Downs Syndrome further back, who caught my eye with his infectious grin and enthusiastic applause. An older woman sat at the back with some breathing apparatus that gurgled periodically. Everyone in the room seemed to be having a great time.

I liked to mix up the solo set and throw in some slow, emotional songs between the more raucous sing-along ones. Halfway through my first set, I could feel I had the audience in the palm of my hand. I was just at the moment of pouring my heart out and laying my soul bare. I could see everyone in the room was thoroughly engaged and hanging off my every word when Diesel strutted before me and took a giant shit on the carpet.

The vibe in the room turned on a dime. Hilarity ensued as Kate turned scarlet and ushered Diesel out of the room. John and the gentleman wearing the trilby tried to clean up the mess, filling the room with pine-scented air freshener and apologising profusely for the unexpected intermission.

Dog poop aside, the gig had gone pretty well, and I'd enjoyed everyone's company immensely as I'd gotten to know various characters in the break. After the gig, Diesel and I were exhausted and ready to sleep, but it seemed like the party was only just getting started in Kate and John's little Bohemian-looking mid-terrace living room. I wondered what their neighbours felt about this and was promptly introduced to them. I guess they're okay with the noise, then.

After an hour of politely propping my eyelids open, I realised I was starting to lose whole swathes of people's sentences and took John to one side, asking if he'd mind terribly if I disappeared off to my room, lightweight that I am.

John shuffled around awkwardly and pointed to the sofa in the middle of the room,

'It's a sofa bed,' he said, '*This* is your room.'

'Ah,' I replied, realising I was in for the long haul. I decided to roll up my eyelids and try my best to stay awake for a little longer.

Four hours later, the party was still raging. I curled up on the sofa and patted it, looking for Diesel to join me. We both snuggled down and made the best of it. I drifted in and out of consciousness until, at about 6 a.m., the last guests finally left. Diesel and I slept a solid hour before my alarm went off, reminding me that I had a five-hour drive and another gig to do later that day.

Nose-mining crotch goblins and a Michelin-star restaurant

Early in my music career, I took almost any gig I could and worked with as many different bands as possible to keep the bills paid. This meant I often played a different set and genre several times a week. I loved the challenge. One day, I'd be playing a gentle smooth jazz set for people to ignore while they ate their Sunday roasts; the next day, I'd be playing into the wee hours of the morning in a sweaty rock band. Another day would be a folk festival, and the next, a wedding. On this occasion, I was playing a smooth jazz gig in the afternoon and a blues-rock gig the same evening.

Playing a Michelin-star restaurant on the Welsh border, our remit was to play some 'unobtrusive jazz' to the posh diners. When we arrived, the servers were dressed extremely formally, and it felt like we'd be playing to some super-rich A-listers. The meals came out from the kitchen, and we could hear every table 'ooh' and 'aah' at the immaculate presentation of each meticulously arranged plate.

The menu was so pompous that I needed to google every other word. Why say *'compote'* when you mean *'jam?'* Why say *'crudités'* when you mean 'we couldn't be bothered to cook this.' And don't even get me started on your *'amuse-bouches'* and your *'red wine reductions.'* *'Minced and reformed beef in a sumptuous patty, cooked and placed inside a lightly crusted gluten-free brioche bun, along with delicately wilted seasonal vegetables and a zesty tomato coulis served with a side of deep-fried, finger-length slices of Yukon Gold potato.'* Burger and fries for fucks sake.

We set up in the corner of the restaurant, and although we were getting a fixed fee for the gig, the landlord had also given us a tip jar to put in front of us. The clientele was wealthy, and we were not, so it seemed to make sense. We put a few notes and coins in ourselves to encourage people to be generous.

As people arrived, it was evident the clientele was not only wealthy, but they desperately needed us to know they were. One portly gentleman stood by our set-up and opened his wallet, displaying probably about 500 pounds worth of twenty-pound notes. Then, ensuring we'd seen his somewhat vulgar display of wealth, he closed the wallet, reached into his pocket and put 10p in the tip jar, smirking and snorting to himself as he waddled to his table.

When we were just about to start playing, one of the servers ushered in a family with two small children and sat them directly in front of us. The whining commenced almost immediately. This wasn't the kind of restaurant to provide treasure maps and crayons to entertain the kids. These little darlings intended to let everyone in a five-mile radius know this was unacceptable.

The sound of two children hellbent on screaming was enough to make the testicles of every man in the restaurant shrink into their bodies. The children's screams were bloodcurdling, and if you didn't know that they'd been simply asked to sit still, you would honestly think they were being murdered. They really didn't blend well with our dinner jazz setlist.

Eventually, the scarlet colours of the parents' cheeks reached rush-to-hospital-fever shades, and the children were allowed to get down from the table and disappear off to pester the other diners. No longer the parents' problem, or ours, we managed to play a couple of songs with the children's yelps as background (rather than foreground) noise before they returned. Then, with her fancy chiffon and lace baby-pink dress tucked firmly in her knickers, the elder child searched around for something to do and decided that our tip jar was the most exciting thing in the room.

The younger boy stood in front of me, repeatedly picking his nose, inspecting it and positively gorging himself on the bogey bank he'd unearthed. I guess the menu wasn't up to his standards. Turning round to gauge his parents' level of interest, he reached his pudgy little hand into the jar and pulled out the five-pound note I'd just put in. Looking at me as if to say, 'I know I shouldn't be doing this, but what you gonna do about it?' he then trotted back to his mum and handed her the cash. Mum absentmindedly took the money from the boy without even making eye contact and put it in her pocket. The miserable child was obviously frustrated that this hadn't gotten mummy's attention, so he returned to the scene of the crime to take out a few coins. At the end of a song, I called to the mother over the microphone, and she looked down her nose so far that she almost went cross-eyed. Other customers were starting to look, and Mum had turned that delightful shade of scarlet again, so I stepped away from the mic to her table and quietly repeated what had happened.

'And...?' she said, pushing her 'organic pan-fried succulent pieces of boneless chicken marinated in ginger and garlic, spiced with freshly pounded black peppercorns, gram flour and chargrilled with locally sourced egg yolk' around the plate nonchalantly.

'And I will need him to put it back in the jar, please,' I said, in a voice that I hoped made it clear that my response wasn't a request.

'We don't like to discipline our children; it's not good for their morale. So he will when he's ready, perhaps.'

I shook my head and wandered back to the stage. I had a job to do and couldn't be bothered with this. I'd deal with it after the gig.

By the time the gig was over, the tip jar was empty. Every time someone came by and added to it, it was a race between me and the thieving little crotch-goblin to see whose money it would become. Every time he would swoop in just as both my hands were busy. Each time, he wandered proudly back to his mother, who ignored the child and absentmindedly put the cash into her pocket.

Halfway through our second set, the servers were called to the other side of the restaurant to perform some kind of elaborate flambé ritual with some whiskey and blackberries and a table full of delighted foodies. At this exact moment, the family who had been the bane of my existence all afternoon decided to put down their deluxe silver cutlery, throw their Egyptian cotton serviettes onto the floor, and leg it.

We played a Bikers Club that evening—a dark, seedy-looking dive bar with around 200 leather-clad tattooed men and women. I cannot fault their behaviour at any point during the evening. They were a positive delight.

Dog snuggles and moonshine

'What would you like for breakfast tomorrow, Sarah?' asked the guy behind the bar. 'You're my first-ever overnight guest, and I wanna make sure I get it right. We don't want no bad Tripadvisor reviews, do we?'

'You can have freshly baked waffles, or a full Scottish breakfast or porridge or...' he paused and looked skyward, 'whatever you want, your presence is a big deal to me, and I wanna get it right,' he reiterated.

'You're my first evvverrrrr overnight guest,' said the guy again, drawing out the word 'ever' to make it seem like it really was quite a big deal. I didn't catch his name then, but I was sure we'd have time to chat over breakfast the following day. If nothing else, I wanted to quiz him on how a guy with a strong Southern States accent had come to live in a rural part of Scotland with less than 8,000 inhabitants. Perhaps it was because there were almost 20 pubs within walking distance?

After a very brief breakfast-orientated chat, I left the pub, telling the guy I'd be back after the gig and thanking him in advance for his hospitality. Then I pootled off down the road to the venue, I met the promoter for the gig: an older gentleman, perhaps in his mid-70s. I'd spoken with him several times on the phone, and we'd connected on Facebook. I liked him. He seemed really genuine and with a great sense of humour. I knew we were going to get along just great.

My expectations of Robin were exceeded. He was a wonderfully kind man with a heart of gold. He was no taller than me and had long, flowing, curly silver hair that made him look like an extra from *Lord Of The Rings*. He drove us to a picturesque little café and treated me to lunch. We sat in the harbour café, swilling mugs of hot tea and burning the roofs of our mouths on toasted cheese sandwiches. Looking out over the North Sea, we enjoyed our lunch as though we'd known each other for years. There was a familiarity about Robin that put me at ease. His wife, Annie, joined us as we were finishing up our toasties, and the two of them spent the afternoon giving me a guided tour of the village, delighting in teaching me its history and gossip.

The gig was superb. Absolutely superb. Because Robin and Annie were having some work done at their house, they'd arranged for me to be the 'first evverrrr overnight guest' with the Southern States guy. I mourned the fact that I wouldn't be able to spend the evening after the gig with Robin and Annie - I'd felt so comfortable with them - but they'd promised to be at the pub in the morning to join me for breakfast. They'd even agreed to bring their three dogs with them. There's nothing better than dog snuggles when you're on tour and away from everything familiar to you.

After the gig, Robin, Annie, I and a few audience members went back to the pub for a nightcap. It was in a pretty run-down-looking place, but its location more than made up for that. Sat atop a hill with a commanding view of the village in one direction and the North Sea in the other, the pub was bathed in a glorious orange as the sun was heading to bed when we arrived. It was mid-summer, and it is often past 11 p.m. in the North of Scotland before the sun truly sets. The colours were spectacular, and capturing the scene on my pathetic-number-of-pixels flip phone was impossible. So I did my best to capture the scene in my brain and store it for later before I followed Robin into the pub.

Already tired from a long drive, a tour of the village, and an enthusiastic audience, I had plans to follow the sun straight to bed after a quick-enough-not-to-be-rude pint with everybody. But, on entering the pub, it was suddenly brought to my attention that my plans were about to be thwarted. The place was heaving! I have no idea how a village that size could have that many people in one of its 20 pubs at 11 p.m., but there we were, standing shoulder to shoulder with people screaming their drinks orders over the deafeningly thump-thump-thump of what I call shed-building music.

Robin got us some drinks and ushered us to the quietest corner of the pub he could find. Once seated, he began shouting at the top of his voice directly in my ear. I caught every third or fourth word and hoped that I was nodding in the right places. I was already fighting off a bit of a cold after a punishing week of gigs and travelling and was in no frame of mind to be shouting. I smiled and nodded as much as I could, hoping beyond hope that he wasn't telling me some gruesome tale of a grizzly murder or a terrible loss because, honestly, I'd have been making quite an enemy with my smiling and nodding without having any clue.

Before long, I was close to finishing my drink when Robin decided it was time for me to get to know the landlord. So, disappearing off to find him, I hoped beyond hope that the guy would return, see my heavy eyelids, take pity and show me to my room.

Robin returned with the landlord I'd met earlier. I'd guess he was in his sixties. He introduced himself to me as 'Aruba,' or at least I think that's what he said; it was impossible to tell it was so loud. Aruba had a black and white skull-and-crossbones bandana tied around his obviously thinning hair. Some straggly, unnatural-looking, dyed jet-black strands fell haphazardly over his shoulders like wayward last-ditch attempts at youth. Little frayed bootlaces of hope clinging desperately to the head of a man whose scalp had other ideas. Aruba wore a scarlet red satin shirt sporting some large damp pit stains. His trousers were tight black leather, and on his feet were a pair of almost laughably bad plasticky-looking cowboy boots that looked left over from a hastily thrown-together fancy dress outfit.

Aruba was a Kentucky-born man who had decided one day to leave it all behind and run a pub in rural Scotland. He told me that he'd been in a band, but it had gotten too much for him. Judging by the air guitar gestures, I think that's what he said anyway. The peace and tranquillity of Scotland had wooed him on a holiday; he'd sold everything and never returned to America. Casting my tired eyes around the deafeningly loud pub teeming with underage drinkers, I wondered if his definition of tranquillity might be a little different to mine.

Between beats in the music, I managed to yell enough to ask him when the pub closed because I was ready to head up and get some sleep.

'Not til midnight,' said Aruba, grinning and downing another shot of something he'd brewed himself.

'It's OK, Sarah,' I thought, *'just one more hour, and you can get some rest.'*

I decided to do my best to win Aruba over, so I ordered another round and one for him of whatever fucked up shit he was drinking, positioning myself so I could see the clock on the wall behind Robin, hopefully without being too obvious.

Midnight came and went. The party was still very much in full swing and showing no signs of slowing down.

One o'clock came and went. By this time, I could feel myself swaying and shaking with tiredness. I'm not a night owl at the best of times, but I'd been up since 5 am and had had a damn busy day.

Annie noticed I was fading and decided it was time to call it a night. She managed to drag Aruba away from whatever the hell it was that he was drinking to show me to my room, and she bid me goodnight, promising to see me in the morning for the pre-arranged doggy-snuggle breakfast date.

Upon opening the door to my sanctuary for the night, I realised my room was directly above the bar. The noise of the drums and bass was thudding up through the floor and shaking the pictures on the wall. I tried to reassure myself by thinking that it couldn't be much longer and that at least I was lying down and sort of resting.

By 2 a.m., the party had gotten louder. It was so loud in my room that I couldn't even hear the conversation I was playing out in my head. I needed to get to sleep. I was due another long drive the next day. I was a little bit tipsy, and I was just exhausted. I knew I needed to go and appeal to Aruba to turn the music down.

I played out the conversation in my head for about half an hour. In part, I was hoping that the music would just stop and, in part, dreading the idea of confrontation - especially in my pastel blue fuzzy bunny pyjamas. Reasoning with myself, I figured it might make more impact if I went downstairs in my pyjamas rather than getting dressed. I hoped Aruba might take pity and he'd turn the music down. It wasn't a huge ask. In fairness, I'd have been happy to join in any other night, but when I'm tired, I'm tired, and there's no fixing that without sleep.

I pulled open the door to my room and made my way back down the stairs. I didn't care who saw me. They were pretty cute pyjamas, and I had a point to make.

As soon as I stepped into the bar, Aruba saw me. A remorseful look washed over his face, and he instantly turned the stereo off. He nodded slowly at me, his lips pursed tight and his eyes shut. I thanked him profusely and set off back up the stairs.

The second I closed my door, the music started again. There was a huge cheer and a chant of 'drink, drink, drink'. The music was even louder than before. At the end of the chanting, the bar erupted into a deafening cacophony of underage drinkers, all vying for their place in tomorrow's *World's Worst Hangover* competition.

At 4.30 a.m., there was still no let-up, so I went back down the stairs. Aruba instantly turned the music off, and the kids all made a kind of taunting 'ner-ner-na-ner-ner,' noise in my direction.

Aruba stood pointing at me until everyone in the bar was watching. Despite my previous convictions, I started to wonder if bringing my fuzzy blue bunny pyjamas to the party had been a terrible idea. The silence I'd been craving was deafening.

'You,' he slurred, 'get out. Go on, get the fuck out of my pub. You're not welcome here.'

The teenagers cheered. I'm not entirely sure where he expected me to go at 4.30 a.m. in a small village, having had too much to drink to consider myself safe to drive, so I raised both hands in a (hopefully) pacifying manner and retraced my steps back to my room.

Aruba followed me. By now, I was feeling incredibly unsafe and vulnerable. He picked up my half-unpacked suitcase and threw it towards the door, scattering its contents across the floor.

'You have five minutes,' he said, slamming the door behind him as he stormed out.

I had no idea what I would do, but I knew I needed to get out of there no matter what happened next. Aruba's behaviour had turned from stupid drunk to violent drunk, and this was no place for me. I hastily grabbed my bags and left, pulling my boots on over my pyjamas.

Of course, the only way to leave was to walk right through the whole pub to the single exit right on the other side of the building. Cue more 'ner-ner-na-ner-ing' and a little pushing and shoving from the teenagers whose leather-clad hero was pouring them more drinks and smirking at me.

Standing outside the pub at 5 a.m., I was at a complete loss as to what to do now. Scared to sleep in my car in case of what could happen once the party subsided and spewed out its over-hyped teenagers into the street, I stood and took a few deep breaths of the salty sea air.

Despite Robin being in his mid-70s, I decided that calling and waking him was my safest and most sensible option. I took an even deeper breath and dialled his number, knowing that I'd have to devise a new plan if I got no answer, and I just didn't have one.

Eventually, after what felt like an eternity, Robin answered. I guess caller ID had come up on his phone, and he answered the phone incredibly chipper for someone who'd been woken just before dawn.

'Hey Sarah, what's up?' he shouted in a truly jubilant voice that belied the hangover he should have been developing. I explained what had happened, bursting into tears as the reality of the situation sunk in. My mind went off on a catastrophe loop and began imagining everything that could have happened.

'Stay put,' he said and hung up.
A million thoughts raced through my head. Was he mad at me and wanted me to sleep in my car? Did he think I was making it up in a drunken haze and I would go back to bed having forgotten it all in the morning? Was he on his way to rescue me like a silver-haired hobbit hero? Staring at the moon, I felt truly lost.

After five minutes or so of agonising, Robin turned up on foot. My hobbit hero hopped into my car, and between us, we piloted and co-piloted our drunken way the 500 yards or so to his house. It was one of two times in my entire life that I've driven with any alcohol in my system (the other being due to hoovering in far too much homemade sorbet before realising halfway home that it was laced with copious amounts of Cointreau).

Annie was up too when we got to the house. She'd leapt into action, military style, and cleared the spare bed of all the bits and bobs dumped there during their renovations. I felt lousy for so many reasons, but the inquisitive early-morning dog snuggles made up for it. All three dogs curled up at the end of my bed as if they knew I needed to be looked after.

I fell immediately into a deep sleep. The guilt of waking Robin and Annie weighed heavily on my mind, and the aggression of Aruba had shaken me. Still, my body felt safe and comfortable, surrounded by my canine protectors, and nothing woke me and the dogs until we smelled bacon wafting up the stairs a few hours later.

All of us were bleary-eyed over our coffees, and I apologised again for my intrusion. They apologised again for their choice of guest accommodation. We were in pretty good spirits, all things considered. Coffee, bacon, and dog snuggles can do that.

Robin, Annie and I (and the dogs) sat and chatted for hours. I lost track of time. They felt like the parents I should have had. They clearly cared about me, and we put the world to rights on every important issue before I finally started making the customary noises when you ought to leave but don't really want to.

'Right,' I said decisively, making no further movements for at least half an hour.
'I really should be....' I tailed off. I didn't want to leave. I'd found a real connection with these two who had become my lifeline.

Eventually, the conversation came to a natural pause, and I decided to do a quick dog snuggle and check social media before heading off.

Out of sheer curiosity, I sought out the Facebook page of Aruba's pub. He'd updated his status about an hour earlier, and honestly, I was surprised that he was alive, let alone awake already.

'Now, before the rumours start, we had a B-list celebrity here last night who wanted to behave like a rock

star, but you guys know me, I won't tolerate that kind of behaviour in our village, so I threw her out.'

It was on Facebook, so it must be true!

I didn't know whether to be big-headed because I'd been upgraded from Z-lister (at best) to B-lister or bemused that my not wanting to party all night had garnered the moniker of *'Rock Star.'*

Making it

I've never really understood what people mean by the phrase *making it*. There seems to be a bizarre belief amongst many people that a musician's sole drive is to *get famous* and to *make it*.

I read someone in a musician's forum on Facebook recently asking that very question,

'How do I make it?'

I read through the responses from fellow musicians and realised that perhaps, just perhaps, I'm not really very typical. The responses consisted of answers such as 'practice hard,' 'get a manager,' 'go viral,' 'play lots of gigs,' keep your day job,' and, my personal favourite, 'try not to let the drugs and partying get out of hand.'

The 27 Club is littered with people that society would say had *made it*. I doubt the people close to them would describe the harrowing loss of their loved ones as them having *made it*.

It seems such an odd thing in life to be driven by. I make a comfortable living as a musician. I have good days and bad days, the good days are on stage, and the bad ones usually involve other things involved in the lead-up to the good bit of being on stage. Whether it's an unscrupulous promoter, a traffic jam or the constant and daily rejections, the time spent off stage can be relentlessly unforgiving and depressing. But the bad days lead to the good days, so I have no issue down here in the trenches, searching out opportunities and hustling away.

You see, to me, the idea of fame appals me. The idea that just because you're good at what you do, you *belong* to the public, and they have every right to dissect every minute detail of your life purely for their own morbid entertainment. No, thank you.

I didn't choose to be a musician. Being a musician chose me. From my age-six declaration that I would be a professional musician and all the struggles that went with getting to that point from there onwards, everything pointed towards me wanting to make enough to live on whilst honing my craft. I never wanted a desk job, although I took one for a while whilst building up my performance opportunities. I never wanted a 'normal' life, although I had one for a while. I realised I could earn enough money to live on to be comfortable whilst tinkering away at my hobby.

The drive for fame will eat away at you for decades. It will gnaw away at you and destroy everything about you that was the reason you became a musician in the first place. Your ego will tell you over and over again that it's 'not fair' such-and-such a musician is doing better than you, whereas, in actuality, it's perfectly fair. Such-and-such is 'doing better' than you because they worked harder, networked better, kissed the right butts, sold their soul to the right manager, or maybe even were just in the right place at the right time. If you let it, your ego will destroy you in this business. But what even is 'doing better' anyway? Surely that depends on your goals.

You won't find me scrolling through Facebook, cursing with jealousy at the latest glowing update from a fellow musician who has found themselves with a fantastic opportunity. Good for them! Some people might scour famous biographies in search of answers only to find that the more famous an artist became, the less happy they'd get, and the more their mental health would suffer as a result of that endless and desperate hamster wheel of being in the public eye. I've been there on a small scale, and it's not pleasant. I've told people I'm doing well, whilst all the while disguising the crippling self-doubt and demons that come with being one of those damn creative types. I've talked about gigs on social media as if they were the best thing that had ever happened to me and then come home, only to cry myself to sleep at yet another disappointment. So, with my expectations firmly in check now, I'm in my own little *unfamous* bubble with no plans to change that beyond perhaps a dream to pay off the mortgage a little earlier than I'd originally planned.

No, thank you. I'm content. I make enough to live comfortably, and I want for absolutely nothing (except perhaps some Karma for the occasional unscrupulous promoter). I have a roof over my head, food on the table, a car in the driveway and people who love me. I work the hours I want, and when working, I do the job of my dreams. To my way of thinking... I have well and truly *made it*. My version of *making it*. Make sure you define your version, or you'll spend your life miserable and chasing a dream you haven't fully defined.

Funny town names and Red Bull

'Ecclefechan!' I shouted as we bombed it down the A74(M). Even though we were only 8 hours and 43 minutes into a 15-hour journey, I was pretty confident I would win the prize for the silliest town name.

The journey had started early that morning in Stromness, a beautiful little town on mainland Orkney. We'd then taken a quick ferry ride to Gills Bay on the very North coast of Scotland before popping in on John O' Groats for a photo opportunity. Arriving at John O' Groats, we learned that, as with all tourist spots in the U.K., it was going to cost us to have our picture taken with the infamous sign, so we skipped the idea and decided an ice cream from the nearby van would be the next best thing. I guess the lady who served us our 99s was used to less seasoned travellers than us as she tried to give us a one-pound note for change. One way or another, the John O'Groats tourist board were out to grab a few pennies from the only visitors they seemed to have seen in days.

We drove on through Wick, through the beautiful but slightly rundown village of Tain and into Dingwall, where we stopped for coffee and the flakiest, crumbliest sausage rolls I've ever tasted at a cute little quintessentially British tea room.

We'd ambled down the A9, which takes in some of the most spectacular scenery on the East coast of Scotland. We'd been in no rush at all: the next stop in the diary was a gig in Inverness that night, so we had all day to stop for picnics, brew cups of tea at the side of the road and leap out to take in the scenery. The gig in Inverness felt promising: the promoter described it as The Best Venue in Scotland, and we green-gilled morons believed him. He'd also promised us accommodation and breakfast before we were to continue our journey south, planning to drop in on friends in Yorkshire, take the whole journey nice and easy, and pootle our way back to the South Coast.

When we arrived in Inverness, we began searching around for the venue. Paul, the promoter, had told us it had a huge *Best Venue in Scotland* banner outside it and was, therefore, very easy to find. Half an hour after the GPS told us in her whiny voice, 'You have arrived at your destination,' we were still searching for the venue. We stopped people in the street. We re-read our email conversations. We even pulled into a Morrisons supermarket car park and asked everybody (including staff) where the venue was. No one had heard of it. Things were not looking promising, and we were starting to feel more than a little disappointed. Eventually, there was nothing for it; I called Paul to ask for specific directions.

Paul told me the venue was directly opposite a hotel, and not only that, it was the hotel we'd be staying in, so we could park there, get checked in, and pop across to the venue once we were settled. He said he'd be there in an hour or so. Once we had the hotel's name, everything was much easier to find, and we pulled into the car park within a couple of minutes of hanging up from speaking with Paul.

This was no ordinary hotel. This was a S-w-a-a-a-a-nky hotel with a capital S. Five stars, no less. Having spent the day in the van, I didn't feel appropriately dressed to march up to reception to check in, but needs must, and I dinged the little bell on the desk and waited for someone to appear.

An impeccably dressed young blonde woman poked her head from the office and smiled,

'Checking in are we, wee lass?' I nodded,

'Yes, please. We're playing at the venue opposite tonight, and Paul has booked us a couple of rooms. We should be listed under his name.'
She found the details immediately, but her smile quickly turned to a frown.

'Paul has *reserved* you a couple of rooms, but they are to be paid for by you.'
I looked around the foyer nervously. A giant indoor waterfall feature adorned one wall. It trickled down into a pond with pink water lilies and brightly coloured orange and black koi carp that sparkled in the light of the chandeliers. This was not in our budget. I tried to look nonchalant when returning my attention to the receptionist,

'How much for a couple of rooms for tonight?'

'Five hundred and sixty pounds.' I swallowed audibly. 'Breakfast not included,' she continued. Doing my best not to faint, I slumped into a dark brown leather Chesterfield sofa and called a band meeting. It didn't take long to decide that perhaps doing a gig for less than half it would cost us to stay the night in that hotel was not good business sense.

'Let's go take a look at the venue,' I suggested, hoping we could salvage some of our disappointment. We'd arrived at the hotel via its rear car park, so we hadn't seen the venue opposite yet.

Pushing our way through the heavy revolving glass doors, we were greeted with a vision of the *Best Venue in Scotland*: an imposing 4-storey Edwardian building with hanging baskets full of long-dead flowers. Loud drum-and-bass-style music was blasting from inside, becoming too loud to hold a conversation in the street every time the doors opened and another drunk student fell out through the doors. It didn't seem like somewhere ready for a live jazz band in just two hours.

I called Paul again to check the venue, the date, the time, and the hotel situation. He swiftly confirmed my worst fears. We were indeed expected to pay for the hotel and, since it was the Highland Games that week, there would be nowhere cheaper in town to stay. There was only one thing for it, and I'm not proud of it.

'The thing is, Paul, I think we're all coming down with something.' I began.

'The other two have a temperature, and I'm starting to lose my voice,' I coughed, probably unconvincing.

'I think we'll have to pass on this opportunity, sorry.' Before Paul had the chance to respond, I thanked him for his time, apologised again and hung up.

By this time, it was about 8 p.m. We had no gig and no accommodation, but we all agreed it was preferable to the alternative.

'Let's just start driving,' I said, knowing that we could always find a hotel or some friends somewhere en route. We'd be fine. I knew it. Travelling the length of the country as often as we did, we'd made plenty of friends at various strategic points between the South Coast and the top of Scotland, all of whom had offered us a bed for the night if we were passing. Now was our chance to find out if they were serious.

We stopped at a nearby Tesco to fill up on snacks and drinks and, of course, to fill the tank with petrol. We were in for a long night. I grabbed some Monster Munch, Quavers, a cheese and pickle sandwich and a can of Red Bull. I'd never had Red Bull before, but I'd seen the adverts and had a feeling I would need wiiiings that night. I never drink coffee in the evening either, but tonight seemed like a special occasion, so I grabbed a large paper cup of hot black coffee as well.

Offering to take the first leg of the drive, I downed my coffee quickly. It burned the back of my throat as it went down, but the sense of urgency and the task ahead made me guzzle it without considering the consequences. For good measure, I drank the Red Bull as well. The last thing I wanted was to fall asleep at the wheel. After a pint of coffee and a pint of Red Bull, like any typical female, I immediately needed to pee. The man behind the counter at the garage yelled 'STAFF ONLY' at me as if it was something he'd grown tired of repeating without realising that it was the first time I, personally, had asked. I was desperate after my caffeine buzz, so I dipped off into the bushes to give a local gorse bush a good watering.

Leaping into the driver's seat, I promised to drive until I was tired. The other guys agreed to keep me awake by playing the *'Ridiculous Town Names'* game, but they were under strict orders from me to nap if they needed to so that I could stop when I was done.

'Wishaw!'

'Moffat!'

We cheered as we hit Gretna Green. I'd woken the guys out of a pretty deep slumber with my 'Ecclefechan!' shriek just ten minutes earlier, so it was nice they could join me as we trundled over the border.

On we went, through Penrith towards Preston. By the time we reached Manchester, we'd passed several friends' hometowns and seeing as it was around 2 a.m., it probably wasn't wise to test the offers of beds for the night. Besides, I was flying with my wiiiiiings and was nowhere near ready to stop driving.

The guys were kind to me and kept waking up periodically, pointing out funny town names, and immediately falling back asleep.

'Lower Peover!' Onwards I went down the M6.

By the time we hit the M25, it was just starting to get light. I was still utterly pumped from my caffeine and energy drink infusion, white-knuckle-clutching the steering wheel and staring out into the night as the sun poked through and the street lights began to fade for the day. I was still buzzing. Buzz, buzz buzz.

I overshot the M25/M23 interchange in my wiiings-addled state and pulled into Clacket Lane services a few miles later, still feeling pumped. Leaping out of the van with the vigour of a runner at the start of a marathon, I dropped to the tarmac and pushed out a few press-ups. Nope. That didn't work. Star jumps it is, then. I didn't care for the funny looks from commuters on their way to work. I did star jumps until, finally, I started to run out of energy

'I'm still utterly wired,' I told my dozy companions.

'I'm happy to keep going.' They had no issue with this, and as I leapt back into the driver's seat again, I noticed that my hands had started to seize up a little, having been gripping the steering wheel since Ecclefechan as if my life had depended on it.

Four miles before we got back to my house, I started to nod, my eyelids suddenly feeling heavy. I pulled over to the side of the road and swapped seats.

'Thanks for sharing the driving,' I grinned as I fell into a deep sleep for thirteen minutes.

Egg sandwiches and scraps of paper

Writing '*Live Music Tonight*' on a scrap of paper and placing it upside-down at the bottom of a pile of egg and cress sandwiches does not, and will not, ever constitute advertising - despite the confused 'we tried everything' pleas of a bewildered promoter.

In the middle of December, we were booked to play at a venue in East Kent. From the pictures on the website, it looked like a great venue. It had a huge stage and function room, and we'd been looking forward to it for quite a while. It was a new area to us, and we didn't have a fanbase there. We were looking forward to the chance to create one.

The landlord, Steve, had been a little unresponsive in the weeks leading up to the gig, but we were more than ready to play on a decent-sized stage, having been forced the previous week to play in the inglenook of a (lit) fireplace in the corner of a small pub.

Steve let us in through the stage door entrance and disappeared off to man the bar in the other room. The first thing we noticed was how cold the function room was. It felt like a night when an audience member might throw me a pair of gloves mid-solo (it wouldn't be the first time that had happened). Steve concerned me by giving off all the airs of someone who liked beer and could, therefore, in his head, run a bar. Somehow managing to slot into conversation within seconds that he was Eton educated, Steve's pink gingham shirt and tied-around-the-shoulders jumper had already given the game away. Steve oozed the characteristics of someone born into money and who had a fancy education but didn't know how life worked. His foppish fringe and thin-rimmed 'librarian assistant' glasses completed the ensemble. Steve was, without doubt, a Posh Twat.

We set up and sound-checked and began looking forward to people arriving, hoping they might help warm both the room and our spirits.

At about 9 p.m., Steve came in and let us know that we 'might as well start.' I gestured to a totally empty room

'People will come through once they hear the music.' He sauntered back to the other room.

So... in a bone-chillingly cold room that felt like a deep freezer on overdrive, we started playing a song. At the end of the song, there was still no one but the band in the room. We decided it was going to be one of those gigs you treat as a paid rehearsal and got on with another song. Halfway through this song, a couple walked in and immediately walked back out again, returning moments later with their coats on.

They sat and listened and could clearly see our morale was at an all-time low. But, bless them, they cheered, roared, and applauded at the end of each song. I changed up lyrics to various songs to try and make the rest of the band laugh. Despite our band-member to audience-member ratio, we were having a reasonable time. Those two audience members were pure gold. Gigs like this are tough, and having just one or two people rooting for you is a mental-health make-or-break moment. Thank you both!

We announced we'd be taking a quick break, and we and both the audience shuffled out through the double doors into a hallway and then through another set of double doors into the main bar. It was at this point that our morale went through the floor.

The bar was toasty warm, with a vast open fire in the corner. The stereo was on full blast through speakers hanging from the ceiling, shaking the room with the volume. The pub lounge was elbow to elbow with drinkers screaming at the top of their voices, trying to be heard above the music. Free snacks in the form of miniature scotch eggs, vol-au-vents, sandwiches and crisps were laid out on the bar for all to help themselves, and the whole place was decorated from floor to ceiling with gaudy Christmas lights and every shade of tinsel imaginable.

On the bar was a wicker basket with napkins and paper plates. I picked up a paper plate and helped myself to a couple of sandwiches. As I did, I noticed a scrap of paper at the bottom with ink bleeding through it from the other side. Turning the paper the other way up to read it correctly, I saw the words *Live Music Tonight*.

This. This was the extent of the advertising that Steve had done. I doubt whether anyone in the bar knew we were playing. So, between the band and the two audience members, we started talking to people to let them know of our existence. My suspicions were indeed correct. No one knew we were there.

Thanks to our efforts and our wonderful pair of new-found fans, we persuaded about half of the bar to come through for the second set. Sadly, not enough people to warm the room and not enough to convince Steve that the cost of putting the heating on in there was worth his while.

At the end of the gig, we'd won every single audience member with our stoic approach to playing in a freezer. Some of those fans still keep in touch to this day.

Steve had no issue paying the paltry fee that we'd agreed to but confided in us that despite his best efforts, live music 'isn't a thing in these parts.' He was thinking of calling it quits and couldn't for the life of him imagine what more he could have done to advertise the gig.

Flying Beatrix Potter figurines, Boiled Beef and Carrots

'If I get another Mrs Fucking-Tiggy-Winkle thrown at me, I quit.'

A freckle-faced whirlwind of a teenage girl barged past me in the foyer, leapt on her boy's racer, and pedalled off into the rain.

'Hi,' I said cautiously to a passing nurse, as my face must have betrayed my confusion at the young girl's departure. 'I'm here to entertain the residents,' I motioned to my suitcase PA and bags.

'Ah, you must be Sarah; yes, we've been looking forward to hearing you,' she said, picking up one of my bags to help show me to my audience.

'Don't mind young Sarah,' she said, grinning, 'she works with the art therapist. It's her job to make the plaster cast models for painting, and for some reason, the Beatrix Potter models seem to cause the most frustration among the residents.'

I'd been hired to entertain the residents of a nursing home for an hour on a Tuesday morning. It was a sweet gig: all done by lunchtime with tea and biscuits on hand for after the gig. I'd been asked to learn a few war songs. The residents loved to sing along, and I was guaranteed a captive audience because, as they'd told me on the phone, most of the residents were in wheelchairs, so once the brakes were on, they were there to be entertained, whether they liked it or not.

I actually ended up playing several nursing homes over the space of about two years. It seemed a waste to learn that many different songs I would have no use for elsewhere, and the residents seemed to light up when they heard songs from their childhoods. I have never sung Boiled Beef and Carrots before or since, but it was always the favourite, no matter which home I played in.

Each residential home had varying levels of care, and had I been older and wiser, I know now I would have reported several of them to the authorities for woeful neglect. All but one of the homes I performed in had varying levels of *Eau De Urine*. There were times when the smell was so overpowering as I walked in the door that I feared I wouldn't be able to sing. My desire to breathe had been completely removed.

This particular home was by far my favourite and the one I wanted to sign up for when my time came. Always busy with activities: arts and crafts, music, history talks and magic shows, this was a home where the expressions on the faces of the residents were of people who felt at home, rather than some of the others I ventured into. Some of the homes were atrocious: the residents were sent to their rooms by 6 p.m., and their days were spent sitting in chairs staring at each other, without so much as a TV for company. Their one entertainment, apart from being taken to the loo when it suited the staff, was me dredging up their past once a month with songs from The War. Society and their families had forgotten these poor people and they were just waiting to die. It was heartbreaking.

One of my biggest regrets in life is that I didn't know enough about how the world worked at the time to understand that the treatment of many of these residents was criminal. I briefly worked as a carer in an elderly, mentally ill home when I was 19. I managed just 6 weeks before I was fired for calling an ambulance to an emergency. I'd been left in sole charge of 18 confused residents overnight. An overweight woman had fallen off the toilet and hit her head. There was blood everywhere. She was frantic, I couldn't calm her, and I certainly couldn't lift her alone. I wasn't even taught how to lay out a body, should anything happen. The manager was furious that I hadn't called him first and promptly fired me. But that's a story for another time...

I'd usually set up with a little suitcase speaker system, a backing track and my vocal/sax mics. At ten to eleven, the staff wheeled in the residents and lined them up in rows facing me. Usually, there were several accidents during the hour, and I developed ways of signalling to the staff which audience member needed an outfit change without drawing enough attention to embarrass them. It was a fine line because without fail, one resident, Beatrice, would wet herself several times during my performance and then throw her arms in the air as if she'd just popped out for a Christina Aguilera-type change of clothes between songs. She relished the attention, and we all applauded her each time she returned.

I never changed my setlist in the whole two years. Each time I visited each home, only the staff and a couple of residents remembered I'd been there before. At each performance, I (think I) delighted the residents with renditions of *Don't Dilly Dally On The Way*, Pack *Up Your Troubles In Your Old Kit Bag,* and of course, always ending on *Boiled Beef And Carrots*. It was a fun time, and the sense of community in many of the homes is one which I cherished.

After visiting my favourite home once a month for a couple of years, the management changed, and their hospitality budget dropped to zero. On my last day, 'Young Sarah' presented me with a Mrs. Tiggy-Winkle she'd painted to look like me. I still have it, and I've never thrown it at anyone.

I won't like it

I arrived at a small country pub in the South East of England to play a couple of sets to the Sunday lunch crowd. The place was full of families. It was Mother's Day. I made the mistake of asking one family just as they were leaving if they'd like to stay for the music. The Queen-Mother-look-alike Grandmother instantly soured her expression,

'No, thank you. I've heard live music before, and I don't like it.'

And with that, she spun as quickly as a woman in her 90s could and lurched off towards the front door. The woman I assumed was her daughter flashed a rather red-faced look at me and explained,

'My daughter is learning the violin, and I think it's affected mum quite a lot.' Absolving herself of her mother's remark, she sauntered off, waving and wishing us a great afternoon.

Luxury caravans and heating bills

The money didn't add up. At all. Again. But it was even more cheeky than usual this time: we were expected to donate twenty quid out of our fee for heating the venue. Using some of the best promoter logic I've ever heard, it was explained to us, very slowly and clearly, 'Well, we wouldn't have had to heat the hall if you hadn't been here, would we?'

We'd driven 500 miles to play a show in late November in the far North of Scotland. The promoter, Liz, had emailed me repeatedly and begged and grovelled, saying how certain she was that the whole village would come out to the gig and that she would make it worth our while.

Spoiler alert - she didn't.

Having promised us a 'huge crowd' and sent us numerous photographs of the *Luxury Vintage Caravan* (it looked gorgeous) we would be staying in, we decided that perhaps we could make it work if we could add in a few shows en route, which we duly did. They were uneventful and really nothing to write home about.

Liz introduced herself and fussed around us like a mother hen on the morning the farmer decides he wants eggs for breakfast. Dressed in clothes fit for a 70-year-old, Liz was the human embodiment of the word 'frump.' Sporting a waxed jacket and a tweed skirt with a matching baby pink twinset jumper and cardigan, Liz could only have been about 40 at most. She dressed like she was the sort of person who would be in charge of village events, but only hadn't gotten the memo that it wasn't 1950.

To be fair, the show itself went well. In this isolated little community, people came out in their droves. I'm guessing more for human contact than for the fact that there was a band playing. Nevertheless, the audience was responsive, and just as we finished our encore, a group of about fifteen middle-aged women arrived and demanded that we play at least one or two more songs. In exchange, they offered to pay the full ticket price. How could we refuse? They tottered in and stood at the back of the room.

As we started the first of these extra encores, it became apparent that this charming group of women was more than a little tipsy. Perhaps the village pub had just closed. They *joined in* with a song they didn't know, and then after that, they immediately began loudly enquiring where the bar was. There wasn't one. They declared even more loudly that they couldn't possibly enjoy any kind of music without alcohol and left.

As we were packing up, Liz handed me an envelope of cash. The numbers didn't add up. Not even slightly. The money was less than half what we were expecting, and her barely audible response as she shuffled from one foot to the other and avoided eye contact was, ' There weren't many people here tonight.'

Bullshit. That quaint little village hall held about 150. Every seat in the house had had a bum on it all evening.

As is often the case with a promoter that has every intention of screwing the band over, we were to be hosted by Liz that evening. In these situations, if you speak up, you end up without a bed for the night so we kept quiet and consoled ourselves with thoughts of the *Luxury Vintage Caravan.*

It was just past midnight when we pulled through the farm's gates. The moon was full, and the farm smelled exactly as you would expect. Liz greeted us at our van and asked if we remembered bringing our Wellington boots. My brow furrowed, confused by her question. Her next question concerned me further;

'Do you have head torches?' She marched off into the darkness, away from the house, with a beckoning gesture.

We hastily followed Liz's fast pace. Fooled by the tweed and twinset, she'd seemed like a frail little old lady all evening. She was now strutting with the confidence of someone wearing a head torch who had walked across this particular field a million times in the darkness. Still wearing my stage outfit and walking only by the light of her head torch far ahead, I was not quite so swift.

Eventually, we arrived at what I can only describe as the most disappointing accommodation I have ever been offered. And that is saying something for a touring musician. I'll grant her... the caravan was indeed *vintage,* but *luxurious* was stretching it. I have no idea where the photographs of the

Luxury Vintage Caravan we'd been looking forward to had been taken, but they sure as hell weren't anywhere around here.

The caravan was damp. Really damp. It had no light save the holes in the ceiling where the moonlight shone through. The bedding was soaking wet. There was no heating. It had a funky smell. Try to imagine a cross between generations of dead rats, despair, weapons-grade amounts of mould and decades of cow pats. That.

Liz mumbled that we should go up to the main farmhouse for breakfast in the morning, and with that, she was gone.

So, in the North of Scotland, in late November, we lay down on the wet mattresses, fully dressed with our coats on and tried to sleep. I drifted in and out of consciousness all night. I was frequently woken by the rain tap-tap-tapping through the holes in the ceiling and onto my face. In the words of AC/DC, we shook all night long - and not in a good way.

In the morning, chilled to the bone, we stumbled back through the field in the pouring rain in search of breakfast. We were still shaking with cold as we reached the imposing-looking farmhouse.

The warmth of the farmhouse hit us the moment we opened the door. A huge log fire burned in the corner of the kitchen, and a welcoming orange glow filled this beautiful Victorian home. I smiled and began to feel as though Liz was about to redeem herself and sustain us with a hearty breakfast for the long drive home.

As we entered the kitchen, we saw the feast before us; four packets of instant coffee and four slices of dry toast.

'Help yourselves', she called from upstairs. 'I'll be down later... toasty, isn't it this morning?'

I opened my mouth to respond and stopped just before a second cry came down the stairs.

'It was so warm in the house overnight that my husband had to sleep in one of the spare rooms.'

After much whispering between us, we decided to call up to let her know that we had a long drive that day and would be off now. It was the politest option we could think of, and in fairness, it was totally true.

We left the toast and the coffee packets and went off in search of anywhere that could serve us breakfast.

I received an email from Liz the next day. In it, she complained that we were ungrateful and said she wouldn't be booking us again, but could we leave a Yelp review of the caravan?

Egos and cavernous reverb

We were given the opportunity to open for a band who were huge in the '60s and '70s. The promoter offered us £50, and we weighed things up and decided it was a big enough opportunity to get our name in front of fans who might like us too. For the sake of not being sued, let's call them Famous Band.

We were more than excited about it, and our social media was full to bursting with us raving about how huge this was going to be for us.

Spoiler alert - it wasn't.

When we arrived at the venue, it was about a tenth the size we'd expected, and with our faces very clearly portraying this disappointment, Dave, the promoter, told us that it was the kind of venue that every band plays twice. Once on the way up... and once on the way down.

Famous Band set up first and did their soundcheck. I couldn't help but notice how inattentive the sound engineer was. He'd put so much reverb on everything that even now, after over a decade, I imagine their music still echoes around the venue.

We were allowed to soundcheck once Famous Band had finished. As we stepped up onto the stage, one of the band glared at me and grabbed my arm. 'DON'T TOUCH ANYTHING.'

There wasn't any clear space on the stage. Cables spiderwebbed across the floor, there were microphone stands across the whole of the front of the stage, and a vast keyboard rig took up most of the middle of the left side of the stage.

'Would it be OK just to move a mic stand or two?' Glaring.

'Can our drummer use your kit?' Further glaring.

'OK, got it.' I rolled my eyes. *Thanks for making it easy,* I thought.

Somehow we squeezed onto the stage, me on one foot and daring not to move. Our drummer sat front and centre behind a mic stand.

The soundcheck was as bad as I had expected. I wanted to ask the sound engineer when his dad would turn up, but the kid was doing his best. Actually, he wasn't. He was staring at his phone.

After soundcheck, we headed backstage to be ignored by the band members' wives. Picture, if you will, the Monty Python team in drag. Two of them were knitting, and another of them was reading *Women's Weekly*. One was stuffing her face with the dinner laid out for us. All of them ignored us, even when we spoke directly to them. They were clearly there for no other reason than to make sure that their husbands had absolutely no fun at all on tour.

I decided to wander back out front. People were starting to arrive, and I always enjoy the excitement front-of-house as people are arriving, even if we weren't the reason they were there.

Or were we?

One of the wives stood amongst the audience, asking people to sign up for Famous Band's mailing list. I didn't see her pen being handed over to anyone in exchange for their contact details, so I shuffled over in her direction and stood nearby, intending to make conversation.

Not recognising me from earlier, she asked if I wanted to sign up to the mailing list. I took the pen, and as I did so, I mentioned to her that I was part of the opening act. She pulled the stony-faced scowl that had become a feature of the evening so far and took the pen out of my hand, mid-scrawl.

'Every fucking person I ask tonight is here to see you.' And with that, she and her hand-knitted brown cardigan and sensible A-line skirt that belied her foul language disappeared in a puff of lavender and hair spray.

A sense of both embarrassment and pride washed over me all at the same time. Were *we* the reason people were there?

I found my bandmates and told them. Spurred on by this, we gave the gig our absolute best, despite the ridiculous setup. The audience was roaring. It was the best feeling in the world.

After our set, Famous Band came on. They played for 45 minutes, came off for a break and went back on at about 10 p.m. Almost everyone had left in the interval. There were about ten of us standing out the front.

I swore that day that however well I do as a musician, I will quit before it gets to that. Much as I was on an emotional high, it must have been devastating for them to be not only playing such a small venue but to a rapidly diminishing audience. Perhaps akin to Andre Agassi retiring after losing in the first round of Wimbledon, having won the Grand Slam the year before. Stop before the ramp to the stage is no longer for the equipment.

We stayed to the end, but it must have been tooth-grindingly soul-destroying for them. Dave, the promoter, came up to me at the end, paid us considerably more than we'd agreed, and told us that Famous Band didn't see us as a 'good fit' for a repeat support slot.

A lilac raincoat and a retired traffic warden

'I'll meet you at the ferry terminal when you arrive. You'll recognise me: I'll be the one wearing the lilac raincoat,' said Jill, the promoter for a show we had booked as part of a tour of the Western Isles of Scotland.

It was three months before our mid-June show at Jill's venue, and, having never visited the Western Isles, I wondered why she could give such an accurate description of her attire months in advance. However, having visited a few times, I now understand. Raincoats are a must. Umbrellas are pointless. It doesn't matter what time of year - our show was almost on Midsummer's Day - the raincoat is non-negotiable.

Jill had already warned us the gig wouldn't be well attended - way to set expectations. They'd received a lottery grant to build a community centre with a huge stage and 350 seats. Except the island had less than 300 inhabitants. With only two small hotels and three ferries a week, even in peak tourist season, it was a mathematical certainty: we would not fill the place.

I love the Scottish Highlands and Islands. Something so mesmerising about the slower pace of life, the windswept, barren islands, and the ever-present drizzle has always appealed to me. I have never felt so tranquil as I do on the ferry crossings between the Scottish Islands (assuming the weather doesn't have other ideas).

The first thing you need to know about travelling to the Scottish Islands is that once you have left your vehicle below deck, you may not return to it at any point during the crossing. It would have been really handy to know this before leaving the van excitedly, hoping to see seals from the top deck, only to return without coats, wallets, or phones to be told that we weren't allowed back to our vehicle.

Cue a very long six-hour ferry crossing. I found some cash in my coat pocket, and we shared a small packet of M&Ms between us. For entertainment, we played Eye Spy until

correctly guessing 'S' for 'sea' became just a touch too
predictable. One guy took pity on us and gave us a book of
word searches, but without a pen, it really wasn't much fun.

Upon arrival, we asked for directions to the theatre
from the guy who waved us off the ferry. He laughed at us,
'dumb southerners.'

'OK, you drive off THE ferry, then you drive down THE
road until you see the sign for THE theatre... and you're there!'
I mimed a little facepalm through the van window, and he
followed it up with,

'If you get lost, please come back, and I'll explain again.'
He wandered off, giggling to himself.

The sense of community is apparent everywhere on
these beautiful and remote islands. No one locks their doors. It
wasn't hard to determine who the culprit was if there was any
crime. They just stopped the one ferry that ran per day and
called a meeting in the community centre. One older woman
told us that she'd visited the island on holiday in the 60s and
had fallen in love with it so much that she'd called her sister to
sell her house and never returned to England again. It was so
charming how they referred to the villages on the mainland as
the 'sprawling metropolis' or *'Piccadilly Circus.'* We stayed
with Jill and her husband, who had a beautiful bungalow
overlooking the sea. They told us over breakfast about the time
they'd found a note on their coffee table explaining that
someone named Dave had had a little too much to drink in
THE pub and had crashed on their sofa for the night. He'd
scrawled his apologies on a little scrap of paper and was gone
before they were up in the morning. Community.

The day after the gig, we took the ferry to another
island, and this time, we decided not to ask for directions. We
were seasoned Island travellers now. When we arrived at the
town car park, the ticket machine wasn't working. It was only a
pound for the whole weekend, and we stood in awe of the
price. Nonetheless, we didn't want the van towed away to THE
garage, so we asked a sweet little windswept lady parked next
to us as she was fumbling with her shopping bags and her keys.

'Oh, you needn't worry about that,' she said, smiling as
we helped her load her car.

'Stan, the traffic warden retired last month, and no one's replaced him yet.'

Small town.

On one of the islands of the Inner Hebrides, we were given a guided tour of the whole island. It didn't take long, but we were shown all the spots the tourists don't usually see. There was a great deal of off-roading, and we saw some spectacular sandy beaches and eerie old castles. Being told there was 'something going on down the road' when the turnout was poor was just a touch far-fetched. I wondered if perhaps it was because no one knew anything was happening; even the village noticeboard was bare, but the gig promoter was hosting us, so I thought it best to keep quiet.

Another island just off the West coast of Scotland found us staying in an extremely religious-themed air B&B. Each to their own, but this was more than uncomfortable. The bookshelf contained nothing but Bibles and magazines with religious-themed crosswords and prayer suggestions. Apart from those with gigantic crosses, the walls were adorned with paintings of various saints. Larger-than-life Jesus', complete with very graphic wounds, stared at you from wherever you stood. What bothered us the most about the place was a little note on the back of the front door saying, *'Please leave the cottage as you would have liked to find it.'* We stared at the various religious artefacts for quite some time before deciding our version of 'how you'd like to find it' probably didn't match the owners. We opted to simply leave the place clean and tidy.

We thoroughly enjoyed our time island-hopping but did find it amusing when almost every promoter said they'd love to have us back 'if you're passing' again. Looking at the map, the only time we could realistically be *just passing* would be if we were ever en route to Greenland by boat.

War heroes and smelly armpits

I once kicked the shit out of a frail old war hero and stole money from a tirelessly selfless philanthropist and his community. On the same day. If you've read this far, you're probably reeling in horror at how utterly out of character this sounds - or at least, I hope you are.

There comes a time in every musician's career when it's not just the crippling self-doubt that makes you wonder if you should be doing it. In my case, an incident with a self-proclaimed do-gooder made me temporarily lose my faith in human nature. A kindly benefactor, a man for the people, a humanitarian, a good Samaritan, if you will. Self-proclaimed. Upon meeting this man, I lost my desire to perform, to meet new people, and to ever venture outside my front door again. Thankfully, the day after I met him, I met a genuine good Samaritan who took my broken soul under her wing and nursed me emotionally back from the brink.

I was playing a *pass-the-hat* gig in a small town in the north of Scotland. I was running on fumes from doing a bunch of back-to-back shows and hoped this would be an easy gig. Unfortunately, it was a matinee show, and I still had to stay awake long enough to play an evening show. I'd crammed in this tour's bookings and crossed my fingers for a simple, laid-back afternoon. The promoter (let's call him Jack) for the *pass-the-hat* gig was well-known in the area. I was given to understand that he was a top bloke, and word on his social media was that he worked tirelessly for musicians in the area, giving them performance opportunities and welcoming touring acts as they were passing through. One or two people had taken me to one side and warned me that he wasn't what he seemed, but I like to form my own opinions of people, and I don't have the time for gossip.

The gig I was to play was an afternoon in a small café in the town centre. It was a regular Saturday afternoon event, and I'd been told it was always well attended and with an appreciative audience. I found this to be the case during the first of my two sets.

A large shiny purple hat sat on the table in the centre of the room, and I could see as I played that people knew what it was for, and coins and notes were being tossed in with much gusto. I was feeling great.

In the break, I stepped off the stage and went to the back of the room where a scruffy elderly gentleman, whose breath smelled of decades of alcohol abuse, was standing at the sink. I gave him a huge wide smile and asked him if he'd mind just stepping to one side so that I could fill up my water bottle.

Never before have I gone from up to down in such a short space of time. His face turned to me with the sourest expression, and his beady eyes pierced my soul. He opened his mouth to speak, and the stale whiskey smell was overpowering.

'You...,' he said, slowly stretching his bony index finger towards me. 'You are the nastiest person I have ever met,' he didn't break his piercing stare.

I was speechless. Tears formed in my eyes. What on earth had I done to deserve this? I'd never met the man before. Where had this come from? All I wanted was a glass of water. Now I had to muster the energy to be back on stage in five minutes. What on earth...? If I've done something wrong, thoughtless or stupid, then those who know me will know that I'm the first to fess up and apologise, but in this case, I'd just met the guy. I just couldn't comprehend what was happening.

I stared at him, fighting back the tears. I just stared and stared and stared, trying to find the right words to say. I had none. Jack, the promoter, summoned me back to the stage, and I did my best to hold back the tears through what was honestly a pretty poorly performed set. My voice wobbled, there were times when it was visible that I was upset, and with tears falling freely from my eyes at a couple of points whilst talking to the audience, I just powered through.

At the end of the gig, a few people came up and spoke with me. One told me that she'd seen what had happened and that the guy from the kitchen was like that to everyone. She'd explained that something had gone wrong in his life, and everyone knew he was just like that. She apologised for not speaking to me sooner because she could see how much his actions had shaken me in the second set.

Feeling buoyed by our conversation, I approached Jack. He was sitting at the table with his big purple shiny hat and a pile of cash that he was counting out for me.

Or so I thought.

He gestured for me to sit down next to him and spoke quietly so that no one else could hear.

'I know we said we pass the hat for the musician, but usually, the performer chooses to give the money back to me so that I can...' he tailed off, seemingly searching for a reason, '... keep this event going.'

I was 500 (or so) miles from home on a tour of shitty paid gigs, and I could see from the wodge of cash in his hand that the café customers had been extremely generous. I simply wasn't in a position to donate all of it to Jack. I gave him the biggest, widest smile that I could muster and told him that perhaps if I were a local musician, then I'd be happy to give it all back to the community, but in this case, I had petrol and touring costs, and I couldn't do that on this occasion. I placed my hand over the pile of cash and took a couple of ten-pound notes off.

'Put these towards the community,' I said and plunged them into Jack's hands.

Jack seemed pacified, so I asked him about the whisky-smelling guy from earlier. 'Oh, that's just Bob,' he said smiling, 'he likes to tease people. He's harmless.'

Packing up and leaving the cafe, I thought about the afternoon's events and wasn't sure if this was a town I would want to visit again in a hurry. Despite the audience being generous, friendly and supportive (they always are), my encounters with Jack and Bob left a sour taste.

I had no time to think about whether I ever wanted to play in the town again because that evening, I was due to play at the local hotel bar. I don't often take two gigs in one day, but the hotel had offered to throw in dinner, bed and breakfast, and it looked like a beautiful place.

I headed across town to the quaint little hotel. I forget the name, but it was something floaty like *The Hippy House* or *Unicorn Towers*... something like that, anyway.

The gig was great. Another *pass-the-hat* gig and I could see lots of people placing notes into the hat. The more the hat was filled, the more I gave back to the audience. By the end, they'd called for two encores, and my heart was brimming. I was doubly heartened because Jack had turned up to support me. I thought that was cool of him. Especially after what could have been a tricky moment over the money from the earlier gig.

As everyone was leaving, I went to the bar and ordered myself a beer. Paul, the hotel owner, plonked it in front of me and said it was on the house. I sat for a while, smiling and staring at the glass. Beads of condensation trickled down the sides; the precious amber nectar and perfect bubbly white head stared back at me—my prize for a hard day's work. Thanking Paul for the beer, I asked him if we could settle up the money from the gig so I could down my beer and head to bed.

Paul looked confused,

'Jack said he was managing all your shows in this area,' he said, with a slight frown.

'He's got the takings from tonight. I expect he'll settle up with you at the end of your tour?'

His voice lifted towards the end, turning his statement into a question. He clearly wasn't quite sure what had happened. I was confused too. I'd arranged this gig with Paul's wife, who'd already disappeared off to bed. Jack had had nothing to do with it.

'Let's get him on the phone,' said Paul, as a pungent aroma wafted from his armpits, changing the taste of my much-needed beer. Jack didn't answer. Paul tried a couple more times, but there was no reply. Paul assumed that, as apparently often happened with Jack, the good old Glenfiddich had probably got the better of him, and he was most likely passed out in his favourite armchair, nursing his fourth or fifth glass.

I decided to drop Jack a message on Facebook. Either he'd read it now, or he could pick it up in the morning. I was frustrated because I had a Sunday matinee gig the next day, and I didn't need to think about anything other than a few coffees and a large plate of eggs and bacon before I got on the road.

'Hi Jack, there seems to have been some confusion over my fee for tonight's gig. I'll pop by in the morning and pick it up if you could let me have your address.' Harmless enough and certainly calmer than my initial thoughts.

I stared at Facebook Messenger for a while and saw that Jack had read my message and was typing a reply. The dots were wiggling in a line as they do when someone is typing, and I hoped for an answer. Ideally, something that said, *'Oops, sorry about that. Honest mistake.'* That would have been just peachy. The dots wiggled, stopped, and disappeared over and over again as if Jack was re-writing his message in lots of different ways before settling on,

'We're even now.'

What the hell? What on earth does that mean? I typed a simple question mark. The dots started to wiggle again. I stared at my phone. Eventually, the few lines that I have memorised for all time that almost ended my career as a musician came through;

'I expected you to give me the money this afternoon. You didn't. So I have taken your money from this evening. Simples.'

Jack wasn't done with me yet,

'If I ever hear of you mentioning this to anyone or trying to get a gig in this area again, I will...' he'd hit return mid-sentence as if to try and threaten me somehow. The dots wiggled around on the screen as I stared incredulously at it.

'I'm a peaceful man,' he continued, *'but you should expect a beating if you ever turn up in these parts again.'*

Holy crap! I could only assume that the whiskey had gotten the better of him. This was a frail, grey-haired elderly man threatening physical violence to a female traveller simply because she didn't have any desire to be robbed twice in one day. Wow. I broke down and sobbed while still staring at the screen in case the dear man had more gems for me.

The dots started to wiggle again. He went on to tell me that he would put the word out there that I had *physically assaulted Bob, the town's war hero'* that afternoon. This wasn't making any sense. I turned my phone off and decided there was no good outcome to continuing this.

I probably cried off and on all night through a fitful sleep. I was at the end of my tether, having played a show most nights for the past week, travelled a great deal, slept in camp bed after camp bed and been brought to the brink of calling it a day. Paul brought me copious amounts of coffee the next morning and one of the biggest fry-ups I've ever seen. His presence calmed me, and he spoke wisely. I was due to play another gig in the next town and didn't know how to pull myself together for it. I was done. The music industry could jog on.

Feeling fully satiated and a little stronger from the food and the company, I quickly checked my phone before grabbing my bags to get moving. Jack was already up, fuelling the rumour mill with a Facebook status that alluded to a female performer who had launched an unprovoked attack on a frail war hero and then stolen cash straight out of his hands. Oh, please! I'd had enough at this point.

I sent a quick email to the Musicians Union, took screenshots of the Facebook conversation from the night before and decided to leave it in their hands. The M.U. had always done a great job supporting me in the past, and I needed to put this whole debacle behind me if I had any chance of holding it together in front of another audience. I waved a fond farewell to Paul, (grateful I was downwind of his armpits when he returned the wave) and hopped into my car. Travelling Wilburys at full blast was guaranteed to bring me back up again... or at least I hoped.

I gave myself some stern self-talk on the drive to the next gig. I sang along to *Handle With Care* at the top of my voice and hoped beyond all hope that Jayne, the next promoter, was more human than Jack.

When I arrived, Jayne was bustling around, laying out bar snacks and generally looking busy. As I wandered in, she grinned at me, dropped what she was doing and ran over to me, almost bowling me over with a huge hug.

'I'm so happy to see you,' she said, in a solid North East Scotland accent. At that very moment, my subconscious reaction to the events of the past 24 hours decided that now was the time to really let rip.

Sobbing uncontrollably in the arms of a total stranger, I relayed to Jayne how the previous day had panned out for me. Not stopping for a moment, not skipping a single thing, I sobbed, snivelled, wept, snorted and blubbed through the whole sorry tale. I even told her that I didn't want to do this anymore and that I may have to let her down and miss out on performing for her. At no point during this blub-fest did Jayne let go of me. After what felt like an eternity, I suddenly realised that I was still clinging to her arm and that her sleeve had turned somewhat silver, thanks to the contents of my nose.

'Oh my god, I'm so sorry,' I said as I hastily withdrew from her and stood up in a truly British stiff-upper-lip kind of fashion.

Jayne pulled me back to a seated position,

'Honey...,' she whispered, 'I know Jack. I know what he's capable of and believe every word you've just said.' Cue more sobbing. I felt heard, and that means the world when you're relaying a sequence of events that, even to you as you're telling it, feels more than a little far-fetched. Welcome to Narcissistic Abuse 101.

Jayne lived at the venue, so she suggested that she and I head to her private living room and eat together. She told me it was fine if I didn't feel like performing later.

Thanks to Jayne's compassion and kind words, I did pull it together and played a gig later that day. Jayne had made the unbelievably selfless (and financially daft) decision to open the venue to just her friends and family that night. Jayne introduced me at the start of my set as someone 'Jack tried to break.' Everyone in the room seemed to know about Jack and his darker side and wanted to show me a little more Northern hospitality than I had received the day before. Their generosity, both of spirit and cash in the tip jar, lifted me out of one of the darkest holes of my early career. If it weren't for Jayne, I would have quit that night. She is my Angel of the North.

Smooth jazz and dubstep

I spotted an advert in the local newspaper that read, 'Smooth jazz duos and trios required for wine bar ambience.' It seemed like a perfect fit: I was working with a superb jazz trio at the time and knew we could happily play some high-brow-wine-bar jazz for a couple of hours on a Friday night. So I dropped the guy an email, we agreed on a date and a price, and it seemed like a simple shoo-in: potentially a nice easy, regular gig, only 20 miles from home.

It seemed a strange layout: a cafe upstairs, selling sausage rolls, builder's tea and what I call '*brown misery water*' (instant coffee). Downstairs was long and narrow, with a thin bar all down one side and impossibly high bar stools people my height cannot sit on gracefully. I hate these things; I always end up looking like a toddler swinging its legs and whizzing around in circles, usually unintentionally.

Mark, the owner, greeted us and said he'd heard great things about us from other local venues - always a good start, and I felt optimistic about the evening. Mark's strong cockney accent was endearing as he asked me questions like 'ite darlin'?' (alright darling) and 'gis a butchers at yer set list.' His gold medallions, satin shirt (buttoned up to the nipples so that a vast expanse of curls poked through), and giant gold rings on each finger were all a little cliché, but he seemed harmless enough.

We set up on the 'stage' - i.e. the space under the stairs. The double bass player had to cock his head to one side to fit. He spent most of the first set complaining that his fee for the night would likely be used to book a physiotherapy session to iron out the cricks in his neck, but we were otherwise having a great time. The cosiness of the understairs gig didn't bother me. It did make me wonder if all Victorian servants and scullery maids had been my height, and I did feel for the bassist, but the audience seemed very happy, sipping on their fancy cocktails and overpriced wines. (I know nothing about posh wine, but surely once you've had one or two glasses, they all taste pretty similar, right?)

The audience was polite and approving. They talked quietly between songs and applauded in all the right places, including after every solo - the clear indicator of an intelligent jazz-listening crowd. There were smiles on faces, drinks were flowing freely, and although Mark looked a little out of his depth amidst the jazz cognoscenti, he seemed pretty happy at the regularity of cash-register-opening moments.

After about 45 minutes of jazz standards, I announced we would take a short break. I needed to fill my bottle of water, and our poor bassist looked like an hour or so on the rack might be a good idea. So we left the stage and clambered up the steep wooden staircase, through the cafe and onto the pavement. It was one of those blissfully warm July nights where you can't even imagine what it might be like to feel cold. We stood on the pavement, listening to the waves crashing against the groynes on the beach opposite, and everything seemed right with the world. From the audience's reaction to our first set, this felt like a done deal for a regular slot.

Just as we were all congratulating ourselves on a job well done, a deafening noise filled the otherwise peaceful summer air. Coming from inside the café was some kind of dubstep music. The noise was visibly shaking the ketchup bottles on the PVC gingham tablecloths and setting off several car alarms on the street. As we stood, everyone who'd been sitting quietly downstairs sipping their fancy drinks poured out of the door with their hands covering their ears. They looked visibly pained.

We stood for a little longer outside, yelling to some of the audience before all of them slowly signalled they'd reached their deafening-dubstep limits and drifted off in search of somewhere else to spend their evening.

Finding my way back down the steep wooden stairs whilst covering my ears as best as possible was not easy. By the time I got to the bar, I thought my head would explode. I signalled to Mark that we were ready to do our second set, and my entire soul relaxed when he turned the house stereo off. Mark looked different from when we'd arrived: a change in his demeanour was unplaceable. He seemed both calm and furious at the same time, I couldn't quite put my finger on it, but it put me on edge. Thanks to the dubstep, the wine bar was now empty, except for Mark and us, and it seemed silly to be playing to empty tables when only 20 minutes earlier, we'd been delighted with the response from the audience.

We continued to work our way through the setlist. A trickle of people came in and sat at the front, smiling and applauding as we got back into our stride. By the end of the evening, we had a small but very attentive audience of jazz fans who were utterly engrossed in the music and not only called for several encores but also asked where else we were playing in the near future.

The moment we were finished, Mark put the dubstep back on full blast. The horrified audience of seniors left their drinks on the table and piled up the stairs as if their lives depended on it. I pulled out my earplugs (I always kept a pair on me at all times for just such occasions) and packed away as quickly as I could, still wincing from the sound, even with my earplugs pushed firmly into my lugholes.

With the van packed, I popped back in to get paid. Mark handed me the cash without speaking, smiling, or even looking at me. I shrugged, glad not to have to try to shout over the noise.

Hoping for a re-booking (I don't know why - I'm a glutton for punishment), I checked Mark's Facebook page the following day to see if there was any feedback about our gig. It always helps when an audience member goes to the trouble of letting the venue know they liked the band, and re-bookings are so much easier than having to scout for new venues all the time.

Mark's most recent update, posted minutes after we'd been paid;

'Sorry to all our regulars for the dreadful music last night (so far so good) ... we won't be booking them again. Jazz is shit.'

I drove past there a few weeks later, and it was boarded up with a big *For Sale* sign in the window. Mark didn't even last a month for some reason.

A genuine, unedited response I once got to a booking enquiry.

Thank you for your email. We like;

Nothing too fast. Nothing too slow. Nothing too folky. Nothing jug-band-like. Nothing Country. Nothing too rocky. Nothing Hendrix-like. Nothing that might make people say 'yee hah.' Nothing with too many solos. We don't usually book bands with women in, so our clientele probably won't like you. They know what they like.

Pinot, bluegrass and bad decisions

'I like booze. I could run a bar.'
It never ceases to amaze me how many people make this giant leap in their alcohol-addled brains. One moment, you're sitting in the pub with your friends, enjoying a quiet Pinot or seven; the next minute, you're still drunk, but now you're also up to your eyeballs in debt, being screwed out of your life savings by a brewery. How does it happen? Friday night drunken bets, perhaps? Overconfidence in one's abilities, perhaps? Who knows? Whatever the reason is, though, one thing is for sure; a landlord on the wrong side of the bar is drinking the minuscule profits and failing. No matter what they tell you. Pubs in the U.K. are being closed in their hundreds every week, and it will only get worse.

Over the years, I've played in many different bands and many different genres. I feel that it is essential to keep tight as a musician by constantly challenging yourself and pushing boundaries. So, for my sins, I've played rock, blues, country, electronic, jazz, ska, folk and many more. For a brief period, I was in a bluegrass band.

The band had been making a bit of a name for ourselves locally, and the gigs were pouring in. We were busy having fun and double-denim-ing it up every weekend in our straw hats. None of us took it seriously, although the musicianship among the band members was sublime, and I loved the fresh challenges that a totally new style (to me) was bringing.

We were repeatedly asked to play in a pub that described itself as a classy music venue. They offered £100 for a gig, and it just wasn't worth our while. It would be a three-hour round trip for each of us. It wouldn't even cover costs. The landlady was insistent and, against her 'usual principles,' offered us £150 for three 45-minute sets. She'd heard the buzz about us from other venues and wanted in on the action. Throwing in a couple of gigs en route on the Friday and Sunday made for a nice little weekend away, so we thought what the hell, and agreed.

Lyn, the landlady, was a large, sour-faced woman sitting on the wrong side of the bar when we arrived. She had evidently gone through the above-mentioned thought process: *'I like to drink. I should open a pub.'* It was written all over her bloated face.

Lyn sat at the bar sipping, no, glugging her large glass of Pinot while we loaded in. It was a cute little place she'd evidently tried hard to make look like a music venue. Posters of jazz musicians adorned the walls, and vinyl records were glued to the ceiling, along with a few instruments dangling precariously above the stage. I stood warily under the gigantic white sousaphone, the only one short enough to stand there. Catastrophising endless gruesome brass-instrument-landing-on-my-head-related death scenarios, I waited for the rest of the band to finish setting up.

As we started sound check, Lyn approached us, waving her hands in the air and shaking her head.

'No. No. No. No. No,' she yelled.

'You can't play that kind of music; you'll clear the place!'

Charming

What Lyn meant was that despite the Bluegrass demo, the Bluegrass posters, the outfits and the Bluegrass description on all our social media pages, she expected us to play pop covers.

Our drummer gestured at our outfits and our poster on the wall.

'But that's not what we do,' he responded, exasperated.

'You play pop covers, or you don't get paid.' And with that, Lyn shuffled back to the bar to pour herself another glass.

We didn't quite know whether to laugh or look bewildered. Either way, we were due to start playing in half an hour, and some people we'd seen at previous gigs had begun to arrive.

Our set list read like the soundtrack to Oh Brother Where Art Thou. Pop covers were nowhere to be seen on it. But, because back then times were pretty tough for all of us, and having been around the block, musically, we decided to go ahead with the gig. A hastily scrawled set list of pop covers was thrown together from songs that any of us had played at least once before. A couple of us had been in function bands and decided that we had enough to muddle through between us.

And muddle we did! Stellar musicianship and something of a *fuck you* attitude saw us through. In the break, a couple of folks came up and talked to us, saying that our set was *a little different* from what they'd seen from us before. I sneaked a peak over to the bar and saw that Lyn was now on the correct side of it but throwing up on the floor. I guess she couldn't hold her booze any better than she could run her pub.

Lyn dragged her drunk arse upstairs to bed, having vomited unapologetically across the bar halfway through our second set. She didn't make any attempt to clear it up, seeming almost oblivious, ensuring the remaining customers were treated to a delightfully pungent Eau-de-fermented-carrot stench. When it became apparent Lyn wasn't returning to clear it up, the venue cleared except for us and the barman, Al.

Al was a young guy with street smarts and a cheeky smile. Sensing Lyn wasn't coming back, he grabbed the mop and bucket and began clearing the mess. Not before coming to the stage and giving us the envelope she'd left in the cash register for us. He said, given the circumstances, we might as well call it a night. Al told us that he'd never heard bluegrass music before and that it wasn't what he'd expected at all. We explained to Al what had happened, and he nodded knowingly,

'That sounds like 'er,' he said in his South London accent, rolling his eyes and grinning at us. Then, he turned and returned to his mopping, shaking his head and still grinning back at us as we packed down the stage and tiptoed back and forth through the puke to load the van.

The following day, Lyn wrote a scathing post about our gig on her venue's Facebook page:

I don't know what all the local buzz is about the band I had in last night. They claimed to have been a bluegrass band, but all they played were pop covers, and they seemed utterly unrehearsed. I went to bed with a headache. Awful. Just Awful! I heard they cleared the place.

Lyn's venue closed down within the year. I guess she drank the takings. From what I've heard on the grapevine, she bought a house next to Redhill train station: an extremely busy major interchange with trains rattling through day and night. She now runs a dog-sitting service and uses social media to complain about train noise.

Witches, chardonnay and taxi drivers

The music was pouring out of us effortlessly. It was as if our instruments were playing us. I love gigs like this and allowed myself to daydream and float above us briefly, looking down on a job well done. Tonight was rocking. The crowd were up and dancing, the lights were flashing, and the alcohol was flowing. The landlady was in her element, and the cash register was bursting at the seams. We were on course for a perfect New Year's Eve gig. We were on course to ring in the year with plenty of bells on.

Jan had booked us loads of times before. So we knew what to expect. Not much space to play, 1960s swirly carpets that smelled of beer, vomit and Febreeze, and endless requests from her to play Tracey Chapman's Fast Car, just one more time.

We were taking a quick break at around 10:30 p.m. when I noticed a woman dressed from head to toe in black. She looked like she had arrived by broomstick. She was sitting at the bar staring at me, scowling from under her slightly too-long jet-black fringe.

I joined her at the bar and stuck my tongue out, cheekily grinning at her—no change in expression.

'Your music is not depressing enough,' she said as she sipped her Guinness.

'I'm sorry, what now?' I responded.

The witch informed me that she'd come out wanting to hear blues music and that our New Year's Eve set list did not meet her expectations of 'depressing music.'

Staring into her Guinness, still scowling, she told me she'd had a bad year. Her breath was so bad that I reeled away as she leaned in to share the darkest thoughts in her mind, and honestly, I really couldn't hear her too well over the frivolity that surrounded us. Perhaps she'd lost her cat or performed a spell wrong or something. Either way, our upbeat music and attitude displeased her, and she told me she would leave if we didn't change our songs in the next set.

We didn't see her again.

What we did see was an increasingly drunk and hilariously confused pub full of people drinking as if their lives depended on it. At one point, mid-chorus, a man climbed onto the stage to ask me if I had lost an asthma inhaler. He wanted me to stop the gig and give him my undivided attention, clutching my arm and stroking my face. He was surprised when our bassist shoved him off the stage. I waited until the end of the song and announced over the mic that an inhaler had been found. From his annoyance and body language, we could only assume it was an attempt at flirting with me. There was no inhaler.

Later in the evening, a woman came up to me again mid-song and gave me her drinks order. In a startlingly strong cockney accent, she shouted,

'I'll have a Chardonnay and two Stellas, love.' I held her by her upper arms, spun her around and pointed her towards the bar, remarking that perhaps she'd had enough.

The rest of the gig played out without too much further drama. However, my favourite bit of this fantastic evening was still to come.

We broke the stage down, coiling cables, putting everything away into the correct flight cases and putting it close to the exit. Everything was just about packed away, and I was zipping up the last microphone into its case when a taxi driver came in.

'Can I borrow that?' he asked, pointing at the mic in my hand.

'I'm not sure I understand,' I said.

He pointed again, a little more aggressively.

'That. Can I borrow that? I need to call out for the person who booked the taxi.'

'But, we've packed away the speakers,' I said, gesturing to the pile of boxes and neatly coiled cables next to me.

'I just need the mic, darling,' he said, demonstrating an uncanny ability to mansplain something he didn't understand.

'It's not plugged in,' I said.

The taxi driver glared at me, letting me know he wouldn't take no for an answer.   'Sure,' I said and handed him the mic.

'Taxi for Saunders,' he called into it.

'Taxi for Saunders. Your taxi is here, Miss Saunders.' Visibly annoyed, he tapped the mic hard and then banged it even harder on his knee.

'It's not working.'

'You don't say,' I said, smirking, 'it worked earlier when it was plugged in and attached to the speakers. I can't imagine why it isn't working now.'

The taxi driver thrust the mic into my hand, called me a few choice names and walked off shouting into the crowd for his ride. It had been a great night.

Buttons and mood swings

'My mother would be so proud of me,' I thought, as I drove down a single-track road heading into the darkness towards five guys I'd met on the internet. It never occurred to me that I might be in any danger; I'd been head-hunted by Caleb, a guitarist who'd seen me play a festival a few weeks earlier. He wanted to audition me for his band, and their rehearsal studio was on a farm at the end of a two-mile-long dirt track somewhere in the middle of Creepyville, (or something) Surrey.

As I approached the old brick-built farm building, I smiled to myself. Any thoughts of coming to a sticky end dissipated as I could clearly hear a band rehearsing. Man, they were loud! Knocking on the door would have been pointless, so I waited until a gap in the music and let myself in. Caleb hadn't told the rest of the band that I was coming in for an audition, which was news to me. They couldn't have made it clearer that I wasn't welcome.

Caleb introduced me and told the guys his plan to bring me into the band. Hands went on hips, eyes darted, and scowls were evident, but no one actually said anything. Smiling at them, I asked where to set up and watched their glares deepen as I got myself ready, evidently unfazed by their inhospitable natures.

I'd learned every song on their set list word for word and chord for chord. I'm quite the perfectionist when it comes to auditions: first impressions count. After the first song, the atmosphere in the room grew slightly less hostile, and by the third song, I saw the keyboard player smile after I took a solo.

The band weren't yet gigging, but they were keen to take me on and told me they hoped to be 'out there' soon. I had some time on my hands, and it was a genre I'd been looking to develop, so we rehearsed every week for six months. The rest of the band lived locally, but it was a long drive for me, and I began booking gigs for them as it seemed pretty clear that nothing would happen otherwise.

They all wanted to be the band leader, which got tiring. I definitely didn't want to take the lead, but I know to this day, we'd never have played a single gig if I hadn't booked them. The dynamic in the band was so toxic that I moved on after about a year or so. I think I'd be deaf if I hadn't. We'd arrive at a gig, the keys player would yell at everyone, soundcheck and then I'd watch each of them turning up their amps a notch per song until, without fail, some small pub in the South of England was shaking at the rafters from the noise. There were times when the drummer was reaching his arms up behind his head to smack the snare drum hard enough to be heard. It meant that I lived with constant tinnitus. We'd rehearse on Tuesdays, and the ringing in my ears would last until Friday or Saturday evening when we'd gig, and then it would just start subsiding on Monday before it was time for rehearsal on Tuesday again.

We played obscure covers that no one but the most earnest of American blues rock fans would know. I had no say in the setlist. For some reason, whenever someone in the audience recognised a song, Caleb would take it out of the set the following rehearsal, never to be heard again.

Caleb was a funny bloke. Stocky, bald and looking like an extra from Eastenders, he 'improvised' the same solos every single gig and every single rehearsal. He was an older guy who truly believed Freddie Mercury's success was the sole reason his band didn't make it in the 70s.

I didn't really understand the need for rehearsals if there was no room for creativity. We were gigging often enough that they should have been used for learning new songs instead of hashing over the same ones every week and making the same mistakes in the same place every week. What would I know?

Bill, the keys player was a grumpy sod. As soon as I'd met his wife, I realised why. She took an instant dislike to me. On several occasions, she spoke with Caleb to ask to remove me from the band. She didn't want her husband to be around any other women. She'd called me early on in my time with the band, demanding to know who I was. I pointed out to her that she'd called me and that shouldn't it be me who was asking the questions, which seemed to cement her hatred of me further.

She'd grabbed my number from her husband's mobile phone and dialled it because she didn't recognise it. I didn't warm to her.

Bill arrived at every gig in a foul mood. One time, I'd managed to find us a gig in a pub's patio garden. It was a pretty small place with not a great deal of space for a six-piece band, but I'd negotiated a reasonable fee, and the guys had said they'd find a way.

Not Bill. Bill arrived and was screaming at me before he was even out of the car.

'I've brought my whole fucking rig for this gig because you said it was outside. I thought there'd be more fucking space.'

Bill was always moody, but this was off-the-charts moody. Out of the corner of my eye, I could see his wife, Elaine, getting out of the passenger seat. *Ah… it was all for show.*

I couldn't tell you whether Elaine was an attractive woman or not. She was so ugly on the inside that it was just impossible to tell. A bitter and controlling woman whose eyes pierced my soul while she scanned my face and body language for clues about my potential interest in her husband. There were none. He was a bizarre-looking, prematurely balding geek whose personality depended entirely on his wife's mood or presence. As I got to know Bill, I realised he was one of those people who lurch from imagined disaster to imagined disaster. He'd come to rely on me, to talk to me, email me, bend my ear, and generally demand my attention over the latest tiny little thing that had gone wrong in his life. Bill could not cope with day-to-day life or overcome the slightest hiccup. Initially, I found him exciting. He love-bombed me with talk of his plans for the band and the future, and it drew me in. Once he had my attention, he began demanding that I listen to his issues on an almost daily basis. His issues were non-issues: things that were none of my business about his sex life (or lack thereof), and it grated on me that I became the person he leaned on. When I left the band, he threw the biggest hissy-fit I've ever seen from an adult. He continued to contact me for years afterwards, promising the world if I'd just come back and play one more gig.

We got on with the gig once Bill's tantrum had come to its natural conclusion. The sound onstage was deafening. Unfortunately, apparently, not just on stage. The police arrived early into our second set after receiving a noise abatement complaint from a woman who lived half a mile away.

As we stood, being given our marching orders from the police, I looked out to the audience, and a certain movement caught my eye. It was Elaine. Sat at the makeshift outdoor bar, she'd removed her frumpy beige, librarian-like cardigan and had placed it neatly on her ankle-length tweed skirt. Staring at Bill with those piercing eyes, she was slowly undoing each button on the cardigan. Very slowly. It was weird. When she was done, and the cardigan lay open on her lap, she spun round, looking away from the stage, and did them all back up again. Then, she spun back around, returning her piercing stare to Bill and began undoing them again.

At rehearsal the following week, and away from the ever-present resting-bitch-face glare, I questioned Bill as to what on earth Elaine had been doing.
Bill looked at me, crestfallen, with the face of a broken and frustrated man.

'I told her once that seeing a woman slowly undoing her buttons turns me on.'

Expectation vs reality

'The client is estimating an audience of around ten thousand,' she said, pausing on the phone for me to do a little imaginary dance.

'Count me in!' was my obvious answer.

I liked agency gigs usually. They call you, you turn up, and you get paid. Not too much is expected of you other than to slot in and be genial with the other members of the band they've thrown together. I loved the challenge, and if the phone rang from one of the agencies I was registered with, I'd get a little bit of a flutter, wondering what instrument and genre I would have to pull out of the bag at a moment's notice.

Shelley, from the agency, was on the phone, excitedly telling me about a jazz gig she wanted to put me forward for.

'It's a huuuuge one,' she said, stretching out the word 'huge' to try and get me to the point of excitement that I'd already reached without her help.

Shelley sent me a set list, and I knew all but one of the songs on there. I was expected to sing a few, improvise a few, and generally fit in. She recommended I take whatever 'Real' books I had (collections of chord progressions for jazz standards) in case anyone wanted to add anything on the day.

'Perfect,' I thought. This sounds like a lot of fun. I was given the date and time for my diary and tried to forget all about it until nearer the time. Shelley would email the exact location once she had more details.

When I put the location into my GPS, it didn't seem like somewhere equipped for a ten-thousand-strong audience. The Frog and Lettuce pub in the tiny Hampshire village of Blitherington-on-Sea (yes - I have changed the names) just didn't seem like a likely spot for a prolific deluge of jazz fans on a Sunday afternoon. Still, what did I know? I bundled my gear into the back of my little Peugeot 106 and sped off towards the coast.

Driving down narrower and narrower winding roads, I began to think my GPS was having a touch of PMS. There was no way that a giant concert was being held anywhere in the vicinity. The weight of traffic alone would be too much for these tiny single-track, blind-corner roads I was weaving down. I hadn't seen another car for at least ten minutes.

Sure enough, my GPS eventually hollered at me in the Irish accent it had somehow gotten stuck on that I had reached my destination. A flurry of little old ladies bustled around a hastily erected marquee. I could see trestle tables covered with jugs of water and an inordinate number of those tiny little paper cones for people who fancy a teaspoon of liquid refreshment.

I was directed over to the marquee where three extremely senior gentlemen were pulling the 'Real' books out of their bags and placing them onto the rickety portable music stands that almost every musician alive has owned at some point but still has no idea how to assemble.

I must confess, Shelley had kind of gotten my hopes up a little more than an 8 by 8ft marquee in the car park of a village pub when she'd said there would be an audience of ten thousand. But, in true Forrest Gump, *'gigs are like a box of chocolates'* style, I repeated my mantra to myself to contain my disappointment.

One of the little old ladies scurried over to us and asked if we'd be ready to play in about 15 minutes. Her hair was tied in a tight bun, keeping her long grey tresses off her face. I learned later that she was the pub chef. With a shape that implied that perhaps she tested her menu rather frequently, she was about five feet square. A dumpy little woman with a huge smile revealing a very crooked set of teeth and a heart of gold. Checking with the seasoned jazzers (I assumed), they said that we could go ahead and make a start as soon as we got the nod.

Wandering away from our makeshift arena gig, she asked me to keep an eye on her, letting me know that she would point at us the moment she wanted us to start playing. It was absolutely imperative to her that we started when she pointed.

I still wasn't really getting it. The trestle tables were filling up with cakes and pastries, and more tiny little paper cones were arriving. I was bewildered.

Eventually, the chef put her arm in the air for us to see and lowered it, checkered flag style.

'GO, GO, GO.'

So 'go' we did. I still didn't get it. No one was in the car park except us and the collection of old ladies with their paper water cones and pastries. Sparking *Summertime* into life, we commenced on what was turning out to be one of the most significant gaps between expectation and reality of my career up to that point.

'And the living is easy...,' I sang as a sinewy young man in lycra bolted past me. Then another. Then another. Then another.

It dawned on me. We were the entertainment at the halfway point of a Marathon.

After a couple of hours, the stream of lycra started to slow down to the occasional limping hero or group of women shuffling slowly and gossiping. Miniature paper dunce caps littered the floor, and we were told it was time to call it a day. Anyone meandering in now apparently didn't deserve an onslaught of Louis Armstrong.

Technically, I played to around ten thousand people that day. My biggest audience to date. Albeit one or two at a time.

Fascinators and hormones

'Honey,' smiled the groom through gritted teeth, 'Now is not the time for this conversation.'

I'd been booked to play at the wedding of a very young-looking couple on a beautiful sunny May afternoon. The bride's mother had contacted me several months earlier requesting that I play in the doorway as the couple arrived at the reception and then again later in the day during the guests' meal. I was more than happy to accept the gig: I'd be finished by around 6 p.m., leaving plenty of time for an evening gig reasonably close by.

I hadn't been present at the wedding itself, and I'm really not sure what had happened, but the young bride's mascara gave her a definite hint of Alice Cooper. Of course, her red face would need some attention before the photographs, but as I looked at the rather large bump in the front of her wedding dress, I realised she probably had other things to think about. She was either extraordinarily bloated or exceptionally heavily pregnant. Judging by the tirade of hormones spewing from her face at her new husband, I assumed the latter.

Standing at the entrance to the marquee, about to be introduced for the first time as Mr and Mrs Something-Or-Other, the bride was raging at her new husband for some unforgivable transgression that was not apparent to either her husband or me. I could see him biting his lip as she screamed at him.

Once again, almost in a whisper,

'Honey, now is not the time,' as her mother sneaked out to ask me if I was ready to play and if her new son-in-law and delightful daughter were prepared to receive their guests. The mother seemed remarkably calm and formal in the face of her daughter's tantrum. I guess she'd seen it plenty of times before. The bride's mother was just under 5 feet tall and decked out in a midnight blue chiffon outfit which skimmed the grass beneath her, picking up small clumps of mud as she glided around. What looked like a small decapitated crow attached by a thin glittery wire was atop her head. I later learned this was called a fascinator and was apparently a deliberate fashion choice and not the result of an Alfred-Hitchock-type mishap.

The hen-pecked groom and his new wife pulled it together and wandered off to greet their friends and family while I happily got on with the reason I was there.

I often wonder if they're still together.

Bingo and spaghetti

I like to play a game - I think I invented it - called Bullshit Bingo. It involves shouting *'BINGO'* at the top of my voice when I've heard more than my fair share of cliché reasons for promoters being lazy shits. I must stress at this point - some venue owners and promoters are shining examples of their profession. But, unfortunately, in the same way, lazy and drug-addled sleep-in-their-own-vomit musicians give my profession a bad name; there are always a few bad apples.

On one such game-of-bingo-inducing day, I met Jeff. Jeff had been hyping up his venue to me via email and posting all over my social media that you wouldn't find a better venue than his. He told me repeatedly that his venue treats its musicians with respect. In his words, his venue was *Like No Other*.

I don't ever recall shouting 'BINGO' in my head so soon after arriving at a venue, but Jeff had the game well in hand. Within five minutes, I'd heard;

'It hasn't sold as well as I'd hoped.'

'It's usually rammed in here.'

'There's something else going on down the road.'

And my personal favourite, 'Yes, can I help you?' when I first arrived.

These phrases are lazy promoter speak for *'I forgot/couldn't be bothered to let a soul know that there was music on tonight.'* I've come to learn these phrases. They are universal. It's like there's a Bad Promoter Bible or something. Do you guys get given a handbook?

Jeff's venue had enough space for about 100 seated patrons, and he told me his shows always sell out without fail. He had spent a fortune on a PA with enough energy to deafen Wembley Stadium, leaving him no money to advertise gigs or to hire a decent sound engineer. Sound check took forever because the engineer, who introduced himself as Grizzly, didn't know how to plug anything in or how to get the sound out of the monitors. When he eventually got everything set up, he pu so much reverb on everything that I'm pretty sure my voice is still rattling around that town like the ghost of ShitGigs past.

Jeff told me he wanted us to eat at midnight after the show. After a long drive and an early breakfast, I was already hungry, so I told him I'd need food inside me to give a good show unless he wanted me to pass out halfway through.

'Anything would do,' I said. 'Just something to take the edge off the rumbling.' He glared and then spun on his heel to make a tuna sandwich (actually, stale bread with watery tuna on the same plate). Yum.

At 8 p.m., the doors opened, and the audience poured in —all 12 of them. Jeff saw my expression and repeated that there was 'something going on down the road' and that this was the best I was to expect.

Despite the reverb in the room being positively deafening, I somehow enjoyed the first set, and the audience seemed very happy. I chatted with every single one of them during the break—all 12 of them. One told me this was the largest attendance he'd ever seen at one of Jeff's shows. *BINGO!*

Whilst chatting outside during the break, I saw one audience member give £20 to Jeff. I overheard him say I was doing great and didn't deserve such a small audience. The £20 was to go directly to me. That spurred me on enough to give my second set everything my tuna-and-stale-bread-filled body could muster.

Jeff's wife was fucking rude. Whenever I went backstage to fill my water bottle, I was greeted with the same sneering, *'Yes, can I help you?'* She spent the evening in the kitchen surrounded by my cases and personal belongings. She made me so uncomfortable leaping away from my bags every time I came in that I collected all my valuables in front of her and went and locked them up in the van. Apparently, that was rude of me as well. She didn't introduce herself or even tell me her name. I only remember her by the name I made up in my head for her.

After the show, I was then treated to food! Jeff drove us all into town, where it would be fair to say there really wasn't *something else going on down the road*. This town was dead.

Eventually, we somehow found an open Italian restaurant and Jeff, Sourface, Grizzly, and I trotted in at about midnight.

The food took forever to arrive, and while we waited, we sat in almost total silence. It was worse than Christmas with my parents. Sourface kept on about how she wanted wine, but we all wanted water, so she sulked.

'I guess I'm an alcoholic then,' she muttered, looking pleadingly at the waiter and shooing him away angrily.

If you've ever tried to eat spaghetti without making any sound for fear of having to spark up a conversation with a crotchety old hag, then you'll know just how that meal went. Each of us slurped silently, waiting for it to be over. I tried to say something a few times, but the silence I was met with let me know in no uncertain terms that my presence was not welcome.

Eventually, we bundled back into Jeff's car and returned to the venue. Under any other circumstances, I'd have left way sooner, but Jeff had promised me their spare room for the night. So with that, some misguided politeness and, more importantly, I hadn't been paid yet, I dutifully silent-slurped my spaghetti and then silent-stared out of the car window until we got back to the venue.

On arrival, Jeff took me into the kitchen and told me he'd counted seven people in the audience. Take out of that the sound engineer's fee (that we hadn't agreed to), the *Theatre Upkeep Fee* (that we hadn't agreed to) and his 50% (that we hadn't agreed to), and we were left, according to Jeff, with just less than £15 to come to me. Also not what we'd agreed to.

Jeff pulled out his laptop and asked for my email address so that he could PayPal us the fee (we'd agreed on cash). I politely handed him our contract, pointing to the fixed fee. He ignored it and waved it away, closing his laptop and declaring that he'd sent me the £15. Several painfully awkward minutes later, there was no £15 in my PayPal account. He insisted it was there and started trying to usher me out of the building; my promised bed for the night at their house looked unlikely. I was four hours away from anyone I knew I could call on for last-minute accommodation.

As he pushed me towards the door, I pushed back and then sat on the floor. I may only be a five-foot-tall woman, but I won't be bullied.

He'd got my email address wrong. Shocking. So, as he begrudgingly re-opened his laptop, I pointed again to the contract and mentioned that I'd overheard the audience member giving an additional £20 and that I'd appreciate that being added to my fee.

'That's not true,' said Sourface, glaring blearily at me as she finished the bottle of wine she'd been waiting all day for. I pointed out to her that she'd spent the entire gig in the kitchen and wasn't there at the time of the conversation. Jeff piped up that I'd insulted his wife and that I needed to leave.

'Gladly,' I said,

'But not until you've paid the full fee, plus the £20 as discussed.'

I was rather pleased with myself at how calm my voice sounded. Inside, I was shaking like a leaf. It made his high-pitched warblings sound like the rantings of a madman.

Fee paid. Not all of it, but Jeff was starting to get agitated enough to make me feel unsafe. My bed for the night was definitely no longer on offer, and even if it was, Jeff's aggression made it implausible.

As I was leaving, Jeff followed me out to the foyer and began putting up a poster to advertise my gig. He asked me to sign it and to make sure to say what a great music venue it was. I did not.

I pulled away, having made an enemy and taken a grand total of £25. I was tired and emotionally exhausted. I did a quick Google search for the nearest Travelodge and made my way through the night until I reached it at around 2 a.m. It cost £76. On the plus side, mine was the last gig Jeff and Sourface ever put on.

Ham radio and bean casserole

'I can almost touch it,' I said, exasperated that after a 500-mile drive, we were now stuck in traffic with the engine off, just 100 yards from the hotel.

'I bet they have beer in there as well,' said my bandmate.

'All I hope is that they have loos,' I replied.

We'd somehow managed to avoid traffic all day. Timing the M25 just right, we'd been looked upon with uncharacteristic kindness by the motorway gods. We'd driven to our goal destination all day: a hotel 500 miles due North. The first gig of the tour was 700 miles from home and was some of my worst tour planning of all time, but nonetheless, here we were, eyes looking up pleadingly at the man with the temporary stop sign.

The man with the sign was unflustered by our troubles and stared vacantly at his phone while a digger behind him ripped up the road surface that led to the hotel. There was nothing for it: no other way to get to the hotel car park. So there we sat until the man with the sign was given the all-clear.

After 20 minutes, we'd exhausted every single possibility for a sensible game of eye spy. I ruled that HTMHB (Hotel That Might Have Beer) wasn't a fair turn, and we descended into silence for a while; the only sound to be heard was me wriggling around, trying to fool my bladder into being patient for just a little longer.

Eventually, the Guardian of the Fresh Tarmac turned his stop sign to go, and off we sped over the freshly laid, stinky black stuff to the Hotel That Might Have Beer.

It didn't. The bar had closed 20 minutes earlier. It did, however, have toilets, so at least one of us was happy.

The next day, we were up early and back on the road, looking forward to the final 200 miles, the gig, and then a day off on the North Coast of Scotland the following day. I'd been slightly concerned about the gig, as I usually am when working with a new venue. I'd messaged their Facebook page a few weeks earlier because it was rather more dormant than I'd hoped for a venue that had told us it had bands every weekend.

'Hi. Do you need help advertising our gig next month?'

'No.'

This had been our first communication since the initial flurry of emails when I booked the gig, and it didn't entirely put me at ease. I'd asked to be kept informed of numbers because it was a ticketed gig, and we were to be paid by how many tickets had been sold. I'd done my best to get us some local press and radio, and we had a radio interview planned for that afternoon, so I hoped my efforts hadn't gone unnoticed.

The drive through the Highlands of Scotland was, as always, beautiful. It is one of my favourite places to be in the U.K. Driving along the banks of Loch Ness is a spiritually moving experience. Especially if one of the local bagpipers is out looking to entertain passing tourists. There is something so evocative about the sound of the bagpipes being played well, and it brings up so much emotion in me that I sometimes wonder if I have some Scottish ancestry.

We arrived at the small coastal village of Ullapool just in time for our interview with the local radio guy. Jack ushered us into the building, which was little more than a prefabricated 1970s chicken shed. Twisting sideways past bookshelves brimming with CDs and stacks of music magazines dating back to probably the very early days of the station, Jack beckoned us to his studio at the back of the building.

The room was a ham radio fanatic's wet dream. Microphones of varying ages lined the corkboard walls; each pegged in place with primary colour pins and bits of elastic. In the spaces between the microphones were cables galore: most were covered in a heavy layer of dust. On the opposite wall was a floor-to-ceiling shelving unit stuffed to the brim with old tape recorders, more CDs and a few shoeboxes with lids shoved haphazardly on top and what looked like a museum's worth of out-of-date geeky accessories.

Jack's smile was enthusiastic. 'Quickly, quickly,' he beckoned as he handed each of us a pair of headphones and pressed the *Live on Air* button.

Jack introduced us on air, and we said hello into the mics. After our 'hello,' the interview continued with a summary of events in the town that month. We didn't feel qualified to get involved in this section, having spent a grand total of 5 minutes in the village, so we kept quiet. Then Jack mentioned that we would be playing at the Community Centre later that evening, and tickets could be obtained at the door. At this point in the interview, having sat silently, I tried to get involved and talk a little about our gig, but Jack talked over the top of me until I gave up and waited to be asked a specific question.

'Now...,' said Jack into his antique-looking microphone,

'...there *is* a gig on tonight at the community centre'... OK, now it's our turn...

'But you all know it's the last match of the year for the Lochbroom Juniors, and you know they need our support.' He shoots, he.... oh. And with that, Jack put on some Fleetwood Mac and signalled that we could take off our headsets.

'Great interview,' said Jack, without a hint of irony, and gave us the thumbs up. I blinked slowly, shook my head to myself and did everything I could not to say what I was thinking.

A quick pootle across town brought us to the Community Centre. We'd promised to be there for 5 p.m. so we could set up, soundcheck and eat (and digest) comfortably before being on at 7 p.m. Unfortunately, the doors were locked and no one answered our door-hammering or phone calls. Eventually, Diana arrived with a key at 6 p.m. and let us in, telling us there was no need to rush. It always bothers me when promoters say this because they really don't have a clue how long things will take, but they will complain if you start late.

Diana wore a beige polo neck jumper and a slightly darker A-line skirt. A string of pearls and matching earrings completed her look. The cloying stench of her lavender and sandalwood perfume left a taste in my mouth that I was eager to replace with the taste of the meal that we had been promised. We were informed Lydia would be bringing our meal by shortly, and I salivated at the thought. I'd not eaten all day because of the slow pace of driving in the Highlands and the important interview we'd rushed to be on time for. My poc belly was growling like a petulant bear cub just out of hibernation. I could think of little else.

Lydia arrived wearing an orange silk bandana and a brightly coloured tie-dyed dress, her hairy legs and sandals poking out from underneath it. Following her to the kitchen and rubbing my belly, making polite but determined *'FEED ME'* gestures, Lydia busied herself with various pots and pans, promising to have a meal ready for us 'in a jiffy'.

I'm never a fan of heavy, spicy or dairy food just before a gig. I remember all too clearly a spectacular over-the-mic-spaghetti-assisted-burp at a gig in Brussels once. I vowed on that day to be more choosy and to try to eat at least an hour, if not two, before I have to sing or play. If asked, I usually suggest a chicken salad. It's easy for the host and just the right amount of protein and light food to see me through a gig - so long as I get most of the lettuce out of my teeth before I go on stage.

Diana had asked what we'd like to eat before the gig, and I had already suggested chicken salad. Lydia, however, was a vegetarian, so she was busy boiling up a gigantic pot of pasta. Into the pasta, she stirred a tin of tomatoes and a tin of butter beans: the kind that make your teeth squeak. I may have made her uncomfortable by looking so much like a forlorn and starving orphan, but when she dished up the food, the pasta was crunchy, and the two cans of vegetables hadn't had time to heat up in their watery can-liquid. Yum.

I spooned in enough of the misery casserole to curb the hunger and stopped. I remember all too well the Duke of Edinburgh hike I did in my teens where one of the boys got rushed to the hospital because he'd eaten a raw pot noodle that had expanded in his stomach. I didn't want to explode. Especially not in front of an audience.

Thanking Lydia for the delicious casserole (hey, she tried), I wandered over to the front door, where I could see Diana and several others setting up a table. Diana introduced me to everyone and told me that Connor and his wife were the couple that we'd be staying with that night.

I smiled at Connor: a tall, bearded Scotsman dressed in a somewhat dated brown suit and tie. I reached to shake his hand, but he didn't reciprocate.

'I'm not only the person you're staying with tonight,...' he said in a bellowing voice that was too loud for the room, '... I'm also the person that's going to pay you if you're any good.'

It wasn't a joke. It wasn't a tease. There was no smile, no wink, nothing playful in his behaviour to suggest he was having a laugh. Instead, he firmly believed that we'd drive 700 miles to play a gig and only get paid if the guy with the cashbox at the end of the night had enjoyed it.

I must admit, for a venue that so adamantly didn't need our help marketing the gig, it was more than a little disappointing to have 22 people in a room that could comfortably seat 200. My belly was making some decidedly unique I'm-processing-raw-pasta-and-squeaky-beans noises and I wasn't entirely sure whether spontaneous combustion was on the cards for the second half. I amused myself with thoughts of Connor tutting at the mess we'd made and refusing to pay our fee to my splattered remains. The things you daydream about at bad gigs!

We met the saving grace of the evening in the break. A younger couple, Jim and Becca, introduced themselves with grins, bounces and warm hugs. Their positivity was infectious and a welcome change from everyone we'd met so far that day. Jim offered us a couple of rooms for the night 'If things...,' he nodded in Connor's direction, '...didn't work out as planned.' Becca also warned us about Pauline. We were to expect Pauline to come up to us at the end of the gig and tell us what was wrong with the sound.

'She does it at every gig,' said Becca. 'She's almost completely deaf, so she usually tells people there was no clarity and that they should invest in better speakers.'

Suitably warned and warmed, we returned to the stage for our second set. Jim and Becca's smiling faces made the evening for us, but every so often, I would scan the back of the room to see that Connor still had his arms folded and had yet to crack a smile.

At the end of the gig, the applause was so contrived and halfhearted that we didn't bother with an encore and simply thanked everyone for coming and wished them all a safe journey home. We'd seen Connor going around in the break, pointing and gesturing towards us shaking his head, so I could only assume they'd been asked to quell any enthusiasm for our performance in the hope that he wouldn't have to pay us - they'd loved the first set.

I began the fun task of coiling cables and getting everything ready to go back in the van whilst keeping half an eye on the audience in case anyone wanted to speak to us - I was hoping Jim and Becca would hang around at the very least.

Several of the 22-strong audience came and asked why we didn't give an encore. I explained that it really wasn't something we did unless we were asked for one. I always feel it's kind of rude to assume. However, I did learn in Belgium that they don't ask for one. There is no stamping of feet or raucous applause; they applaud the last song no louder than the first. They do, nonetheless, get offended if you don't do two encores. So much to learn!

Just as I started to wonder if there was some kind of special top-of-Scotland rule about encores, an elderly lady sidled up to me and grabbed me tightly by the arm with one hand whilst clutching a pen and paper in the other.

'Your voice was too quiet. The guitar was too loud. You need to eee-nuuuuunciiiii-ate, I couldn't hear your esses', she ticked off each item on her list as she relayed them to me.

I interrupted her with a big grin and spoke loudly: 'You must be Pauline.' The lady looked confused and bustled her pen and paper into her handbag.

'I am, dearie,' she said, looking bewildered, 'but how did you know?'
'Just a hunch,' I carried on coiling cables and grinned at Jim and Becca, who were watching our interaction intently from the side of the room.

Pauline wandered off and probably to this day wonders how I guessed her name correctly. I made light work of the rest of the cables and headed over to see whether our gig had met with Connor's approval. The cashbox was open, so things were looking promising.

'Everyone happy?' I beamed.
'I guess it was fine.' Connor handed over the money quickly, together with a piece of paper with his address on it. He made no attempt to make eye contact as he closed the

cashbox, making a rather swift exit. I'd seen this type of behaviour once too often in promoters, so I sat myself down at the table and counted the notes he'd so hastily thrust into my hands. Not only did the numbers not make sense (they never ever ever ever have when I've done a door split gig at a UK gig), but the currency was in Scottish notes (no problem, they're legal tender throughout England, despite what the girl at the Sainsbury's checkout in Clacton says), a couple of 10 Euro notes, four Monopoly fivers and a U.S. Dollar.

I momentarily looked up from my impromptu game of Monopoly to see Jim and Becca standing over me. Jim saw the collection of currency in my hand.

'NOW would you like to stay with us?' I nodded,

'Yes, please!'

Over a few glasses of wine, Jim and Becca told us how they were trying to get involved in the committee and make it a more profitable experience for everyone involved. Jim told us that they were new to the village, so it may take the likes of Connor and Diana around 20 years to accept them. Still, they were doing their best to muscle in as much as they could and try to make the Community Centre just that: a centre for the community rather than, as he put it, a place where 'dreams go to die.'

'Now...,' said Jim, sipping his third glass of wine, '...how short was the money Connor gave you?'

'Well, that depends on whether you accept Monopoly money,' I smirked, reaching into my wallet to show him my collection of interesting bank notes. Without flinching, Jim reached into his wallet and swapped out all the cash that wasn't legal UK tender. Then, putting his hand up and lowering his head to signify this wasn't up for discussion, he poured another glass of wine.

We stayed up late into the night chatting about what it was like to try to integrate into a small town which most residents were born into. We discussed Jim and Becca's hopes and dreams of starting a small and, more importantly, ethical music promotions company in the town to give back to the community. We talked about life on the road, and I shared lots of the stories I've shared with you in this book. Eventually, Jim and Becca retired to bed, asking us to promise not to lock the door if we left after them in the morning. Despite living there for five years, Jim and Becca still hadn't got a key to the house - a testament to the sense of community they so clearly loved about their new life on the North Coast of Scotland.

I woke late and stumbled down to the kitchen. On the table was a note;

We had so much fun last night. We wish you could have stayed forever. You're just the breath of fresh air this community so desperately needs. By the way... please write a book about your travels.

We brewed a fresh pot of coffee, sat staring at the extensive collection of alphabet fridge magnets, and then spent far too much of our day off mischievously wondering what we could come up with if we used every single letter. Proudly, after a couple of hours, and way too much coffee, Jim and Becca's fridge magnets read;

THANK YOU, JIM AND BECCA. PINK BALDERDASH FORMULA YA FUN WAS HAD XX

A morning well spent, I say.

Dodgy haircuts and wild promises

If you're trying to *make it* (whatever that means) as a musician, please keep this simple mantra in your head, 'Nobody (I repeat, nobody) cares about your career as much as you do.'

As I've mentioned before, *Making it* means different things to different people. I do what I love for a living, and I earn enough to live on. I'm not remotely famous, and, as you can see, I've played more than my share of hideous gigs. To me, *making it* is being comfortable, both financially and in your own skin. It's about connecting with an audience. It's about seeing the world and sharing your stories with anyone who'll listen. I've been bored playing covers in front of thousands of people and invigorated playing original music to twenty people; it all depends on your perspective. One thing I know for sure, though - there are way too many scammers in this business: all eager for their share of your hard-earned cash in exchange for the promise of instant fame and fortune.

I succumbed to far too many of them at the start of my career. Playing in pubs can get grating after a while if you've even a modicum of ambition and if you're approached in a bar by a Dennis-Waterman-looking man with a suspicious comb-over who promises he's a talent scout, mark my words; he isn't. I'm grateful for the (albeit costly) lessons of my early career that I can spot a scam a mile off now.

We called the guy Gerry Combover from the moment we met him, and I can't now remember his real name (probably best). He approached our four-piece blues band after a tumbleweed-like pub gig and promised the earth. Everything from R*ecord of the Week* on *Radio 2* to support slots with some of the biggest names on the British music scene at the time. All we had to do was give him exclusivity.

I was greener back then, and the idea of someone not only booking all of our gigs for us but NOT pub gigs was incentive enough for us to start picturing big stages and gigs where we could actually get the venue to turn the TV off during our set. We were a wet-behind-the-ears easy mark, and he knew it. All we had to do was record an album, and he'd get it to his buddy with 'massive connections' and BOOM, we'd be receiving commercial airplay on some of the biggest stations across the globe. Simple, right?

Mr. Combover drew up an agreement for us to sign. It was an exclusive deal whereby he was to be the sole agent for booking gigs for us. This included not booking our own gigs due to 'professional confusion' with venue owners, who may be contacted by both parties. It seemed logical, and at the time, I admired the professionalism (oh, how green I was). All four of us instantly stopped the daily email and phone call pestering. Combover was to take 10% from any booking, and I relished not having to make cold calls. We waited patiently for the phone to ring for four months with good news.

It didn't.

Give him his due; Combover would keep in touch regularly to let us know that he had a 'bite' from a 'big venue' or a 'huge name'. So with that in mind, we set about recording the album we'd been talking about and looked forward to hearing it on BBC radio, giving interviews and signing copies of it at venues Nationwide.

None of us knew what we were doing. We were over-excited and in a huge rush. The album was done within a week: all recorded in the kitchen of my tiny little rented flat. It would be over a year after its release that any of us learned about EQ balancing, normalising, or even mastering. Looking back, it wasn't my proudest moment, although I cringe now that it was at the time.

At the time, we had the self-belief of any musician with a debut album, and we knew we'd be the Next Big Thing. We had a thousand copies made up and sent Combover a digital copy to help with the bookings. Within minutes he was on the phone. With hindsight, it should have been within 44 minutes (the length of the album) and not within less than ten.

'This is astounding,' said Combover.

'The best debut album I've ever heard,' he continued, and the icing on the cake;

'I'm so grateful to be working with you.'

With our egos suitably massaged, we agreed it was time to get Combover's buddy involved in the promotions. It seemed to be the next wise move.

Combover put us in touch with his buddy. Let's call his company 'Get Fucked Promotions.' I can't realistically name them because somehow they are still in business, and I'd be a naughty little sax player if I did. The trouble with Get-Fucked is that the guy really does have some influential contacts which he uses for his bigger-named artists. However, his bread and butter comes from scamming the little guy desperate for media attention. Do I sound bitter? Hopefully not. It was a valuable lesson I needed to learn and I'm grateful. So if you're reading this and on the cusp of signing with something that doesn't feel right, maybe I can stop you from being the monumental pillock that I was.

Get-Fucked's deal was for us to send him 500 copies of the album, which he would send to all his contacts: radio, magazine, festivals, etc. On top of that, we were to send a cheque for £1000 to cover 'expenses.' It didn't feel right. It really didn't feel right, and even as I'm typing this, I'm bewildered that we still went ahead and agreed to go for it.

We clubbed together and excitedly wrote a check to get fucked. And fucked we got.

The first week after sending the cheque, we got a phone call to say that an internet radio station wanted to chat with us about the new album. Scouring social media, we discovered the show was a hospital radio show with a generous estimate of around 100 listeners. Woohoo! The Big Time. We did the interview over the phone, and the interviewer's first question was, '...so what's the band called?'

After that, we heard nothing. Zilch. Zip. Nada. Zero. Squat. Nowt.

We called Get Fucked several times in the months afterwards, and it always either went straight to answerphone or was answered by someone saying something like,

'JK, can you just hold on one moment,' followed by a hasty, 'Hi, Sarah, I'm on the phone with Jamiroquai. Can I call you back?' followed by the dial tone. We called and called and called and called and called. Eventually, our bassist emailed;

We'd like a progress report. In-person. Alternatively,
we can speak with the Musician's Union about our
experiences with you.

That worked! A meeting was set up for the following
Saturday in a pub halfway between us and his 'offices.' Get
Fucked was predictably over an hour late. When he arrived, he
ambled towards us and gave no apology.

He began by staring straight at me, the only female in
the band, and called me a 'pushy little bitch.' Ah... so we're off
to a good start here, then. When our bassist responded that
perhaps I wasn't so much pushy as a touch frustrated that the
person who was supposed to be pushy on our behalf was in
fact, a lazy little shit, I welled up with pride. Get Fucked had no
answer to this but to tell us that he'd sent our music out to all
500 of his contacts, and not one of them had liked it. His rant
continued... the only reason we'd got the hospital radio
interview was that the guy owed him a favour, we were
clueless, there was no future for us, blah blah blah.

For some reason, perhaps morbid curiosity, we
continued the meeting for another hour after this. We ordered
lunch and made notes as Get Fucked gave us wisdom and
career advice he believed would stand us in a better position
for our next release. As a 'gesture of goodwill,' he even offered
to take on any future releases of ours for the same price,
although by this point, surely even he could see the cynicism in
our eyes.

I made notes on every piece of advice he gave us. He
was adamant about specific make-or-break issues, for
example, the colour of the tablecloth on the merchandise table.
He was at pains to tell us that ours was an incredibly original
band name (despite all evidence to the contrary) and that we
should definitely keep it. He even advised us on running order
and set lists (always start with a slow and mournful song) and
told us adamantly that even if we didn't need them, we should
always have music stands with our lyrics on the stage.

It is entirely possible that Get Fucked realised as the
meal went on that our fawning over his advice had become
more tongue-in-cheek than kiss-on-butt because the moment
he put his knife and fork together, he made his excuses and
stood up, asking a waitress where the bathroom was.

We spotted his distinctive shuffle across the car park moments later as he fled and left us with the bill and a bullet-point list of the worst career advice I have ever been given.

On the drive home, we looked at the list and thought about the exact opposite of every single piece of advice I'd hastily scrawled down. No music stands (learn the damn lyrics so you can engage with your audience), the opposite colour tablecloth, an energetic and enthusiastic first song and a change of band name. It was the shake-up we all needed. Scrapping the remaining CDs, we redesigned the cover, changed the band name, and re-released it (in all its still unmastered glory). We all worked our asses off contacting radio stations, newspapers and magazines. Within a couple of weeks, we'd got ourselves interest from several big-name magazines and more airplay than we could have dreamed of. Many of the five-star reviews came in from magazines Get Fucked had told us hated the music. The gigs still weren't coming in though, thanks to Combover, so we dropped him an email and dropped him too.

Two weeks of hustling later the diary was full. An 18-date tour throughout the UK ensued, and the press got behind us. It was a massive achievement for a bunch of clueless hopefuls with no marketing experience between us - even if they were all shit gigs.

Halfway through the tour, Combover emailed us an invoice demanding his 10% for the gigs that we'd found for ourselves. We laughed and laughed and laughed and laughed and laughed.

The band didn't stay together long after that. The whole experience had jaded the drummer, and he returned to playing in a tribute band. The three of us auditioned a few drummers, but the magic had gone, and we all moved on to bigger and better projects.

A year later, I was working on a new project. We'd spent months in the studio and had an album we were all very proud of and were busy gigging and hustling.

One afternoon, an unsolicited email came in...

Hi, I'm writing to you from Get Fucked Promotions. We are an International Promotions Company with 30 years of experience in the music business. We are actively seeking out musicians just like you. We heard about your latest album and would like to offer you the opportunity to be considered for a unique opportunity...

Chalkboards and Mussels

I spotted a chalkboard outside as I drove towards the pub.
'Hurray!' I shouted as I circled the pub, trying to find a parking spot, 'Rita's finally started advertising gigs!' Drawing closer, I noticed the writing on the board:

Tonight's Special - Freshly caught mussels.

As part of a four-piece rock covers band, I regularly played at a small venue on the South East Coast. It was always a battle with the venue owner because she constantly complained that no one ever came to her pub for the music but also never advertised that there was ever music on at her pub. It felt like Schrödinger's gig.

She often asked the bands for advice on how to get more people to come to her pub, and when we all consistently told her that she needed to advertise, she looked at us as if we'd gone mad. It was abundantly clear that she didn't want to take advice, and even the suggestion of a chalkboard or a Facebook post was met with a sigh and arms in the air and further confirmation that she just 'didn't know what to do.'

This always resulted in an empty pub apart from anyone whom the band had told about the gig. There are only so many times you can drag your friends out if you play regularly in a covers band. You saturate the area, and you just can't rely on your mates to trudge out to every single gig, so you rely on the pubs having some idea of how to get people to come in, but unfortunately, with the British pub trade as it is, the sense of learned helplessness was evident.

After three gigs in a row where the only people in the pub were Rita, the band and a few of our mates, we booked our fourth gig and gave Rita a list of things to try to help her get more people in on a Saturday Night. It was a nice pub, and Rita was a lovely and welcoming lady. We desperately wanted her to succeed.

We'd told her it would be a good idea to mention that she has bands on her Facebook page (surely marketing 101).

We told her that perhaps she could share some videos of the bands she had coming up (surely also marketing 101). Maybe she could put up a chalkboard outside. Perhaps she could run an advert in the local paper. Maybe she could invite local groups to hold their social events there. How about a *Happy Hour*? How about flyers? We devised a long list of things to try over the next month or two and booked another gig with her for July when we knew the town would be crawling with tourists. I asked her to keep in touch.

I followed Rita's social media closely over the next month or so. She regularly put up pictures of the beers on tap, advertised the Monday night bingo and shared news about what was generally happening in town. However, at no point did she mention any live music, even though I knew that she booked bands three nights a week.

I wasn't feeling optimistic when we pulled up outside two months later. Rita hadn't kept in touch, and I'd seen no mention on social media or in town about our gig, let alone the pub having *any* live music. In a town with a pub every twenty steps or so, the competition was steep, and Rita wasn't even throwing her hat in the ring.

Because it was such an intimate venue, we always loaded in the instruments one at a time: the drummer going first so that he wasn't clambering over all of our gear and bashing elbows with us. He pulled his kick drum out of the van and carried it up the stairs to the front door. As he reached the door, someone called out to him,

Is there a band on tonight?'

Standing still for what felt like an eternity before turning slowly and replying, 'Nope,' he smiled and headed back down the stairs, kick drum in hand, shaking his head.

Putting the drum back in the van, he was adamant that the evening would be better spent in a different pub listening to someone else play and speaking to the landlord with a view to finding us a different gig in the area.

We all agreed but decided the courteous thing to do would be to pop in and chat with Rita, and I was chosen to be the band ambassador.

Timidly pushing open the pub's front door, Rita spotted me straight away and grinned.

'Hey, Sarah, what brings you here tonight?'

'Oh, just passing through,' I smiled, realising Rita had totally forgotten she'd made any arrangements with us.

'We must get you guys booked in for another gig sometime soon. How about it?' Rita beamed at me.

I nodded slowly, 'I'll pop back in with my diary sometime.'

I drove past Rita's pub a few months later. It's a Tesco Express now.

Rentaghost and payment in Snickers bars

As I've mentioned, you get a good feel for how a gig will go by watching the venue's social media in the months and weeks leading up to it. That's how I knew the gig at the Probably-Shouldn't-Name-It-Here pub would be a bad one.

Every day, it seemed as though the landlord was becoming more and more unhinged. Every day was a new Facebook update, complaining about anything and everything. 'Yet again, the band played to nobody because you fuckers won't support my pub.' And variations on that theme. Colin was an angry little man with a vendetta against every living soul in the quaint little Essex Village where he'd decided to buy a pub.

Weeks of this went by. I don't quite know why I didn't pull the gig. The signs are *always* there; whether it's bitching at the locals, a website with nothing but a *coming soon* graphic or a social media page that sits inactive, you always know when a pub gig will be even worse than usual. Colin's pub was most definitely shaping up to be a shit show even before we got in the van.

The customary *Live Music Tonight* A-frame board that sits outside most pubs demonstrates that the landlord has done his absolute utmost to advertise the gig (yes, that was sarcasm). Outside Colin's pub, the board read *Closed Tonight. Sorry.*

I mentioned this to him as we loaded in, and he said he'd get his wife to hop out there and bring it in shortly. He seemed friendly enough so far. A vast mutton-chop-style beard adorned most of his face, and a massive pair of tinted glasses engulfed what wasn't covered by the beard.

We were directed to a small corner of the pub where a table had been moved for us to set up. It was a reasonably friendly ambience so far. I relaxed a little.

Sound check was easy, and within half an hour or so, we were sat at the bar, chatting with Colin and his wife. Colin's wife wore an ankle-length flowing black velvet dress trimmed with lace. Her long grey hair lay straggled across her face, combed in a deliberate but unsuccessful attempt to hide a rather large bald patch on the back of her skull.

Colin's rather unnervingly witch-like wife made good conversation with us for a while. She talked about how excited they were that they'd recently purchased England's oldest pub (oddly enough, many British pubs make the same claim). The Witch complained a little about the locals and how set in their ways they are, but it was all in good humour, and everything felt comfortable and light-hearted. However, things took a turn for the downright awkward when she reached behind the bar to show us a handful of photographs.

The photographs were old and had a very 70s colour palette. They were of various renovations that must have taken place before Colin and The Witch had taken over the pub.

I wish I could remember her name instead of just how much she reminded me of Hazel the McWitch from the 80s kids' TV show, Rentaghost.

Hazel (let's call her) pointed to various water damage marks on the dusty, faded photographs.

'Do you know what these are?' she said, pointing to the little round splodges on the old curling photos. She scoffed at me when I said that they looked like water damage.

'Oh, you silly unenlightened little girl...these are orbs.'

'*OK,*' I thought, '*I can see that they're little round dots, and I know what an orb is... what is this crazy woman getting at?*'

'These are the spirits of the people who have died in this old pub.' Hazel declared. 'They are reaching out to us through these photographs to share in their transcendent energy.'

I didn't speak. I was too busy trying not to display what my brain was thinking, furiously stroking the delightfully affectionate cat sitting on the bar.

Hazel then went on to show me another photo that was even more water-damaged. She told me that this was a particularly sad one because the *orb* had another *orb* inside of it. This was the spirit, apparently, of a woman who had died in childbirth at the pub.

'Probably centuries ago,' mourned Hazel as if to convey a more solemn and sombre wistfulness to her tale.

'OK, well, anyway,' I said, leaping up from the bar in search of my bandmates. I know when there's no talking to someone.

By 9 p.m., there was still no one else in the bar except for the cat, Colin, Hazel, the orb family and the band. Colin gave us the thumbs up (International empty pub gig gesture for *'you might as well get started.'*)

We played for an hour to no one. We took a break, hoping that Colin might suggest we call it a day, but he waved us back on for a second set, which we duly played. The gig was far outside our normal fanbase reach, and we'd been hoping to win at least someone over. Maybe the orbs enjoyed it.

At the end of the evening, Colin was suspiciously friendly. He gave us a couple of chocolate biscuits for the journey home and a few cans of fizzy drinks.

I sat at the bar while he fiddled about tidying things, adjusting the pork scratchings display and pouring himself another glass of whiskey. The rest of the band was in the car park, leaving me to sort out the fee and bid farewell to Colin, Hazel, the cat and the orb families.

'Was there something else, or are you all packed up and ready to go?' asked Colin.

Just the money,' I said with a big smile. At that very moment, everything about Colin's mutton-chops face changed. He held my eye for an uncomfortable amount of time, reaching into the till and handing me a crisp twenty-pound note without breaking his stare.

I assumed he was planning to head somewhere else to get the rest of the fee, but no, Colin had decided that twenty quid and a couple of Snickers was plenty of pay for a band who'd travelled a few hours to play for him and his cat.

I held my ground and asked for the rest. We had an agreement, and this was most certainly not it. Everything was confirmed in writing, so I held up the paperwork I'd folded into my back pocket and showed him the fee we'd agreed.

'I'm not paying that!' His face reddened, and he looked indignant at the idea, gesturing around the room at the lack of punters. I hoped one of the guys would come back looking for me soon. Colin's body language had started to feel threatening.

'I can't and won't pay you tonight.'

Despite Colin's increasingly red face, I kept calm, smiling at him and handing back the twenty. Confident enough in my dealings with the Musicians Union, I let Colin know he could either pay the total amount now or the Union would get it for me, plus fees and interest. I was polite. I spoke quietly and calmly. Things had turned nasty enough that I knew there was no turning back. Twenty quid wouldn't even cover our petrol, and I wasn't having it.

After what felt like an eternally long staring match, Colin plunged his hand into the cash register and retrieved the rest of the money. Leaning close to me in an attempt to be threatening, he reached over the bar as if he were about to punch me. I didn't flinch. This angered him even further.

Colin did as all bullies do if their intimidation techniques aren't working. He had a hissy fit. A full-on toddler tantrum. It was spectacular. Colin marched over to the door, flung it open and threw the cash into the car park. One of my bandmates started giggling while he picked up the remaining money, counting extra loudly as he picked up each note. I don't think that helped Colin's mood a great deal. He looked again as if he was about to punch me but thought better of it and pointed to the door.

'Get out and never come back.'

As I wandered back to the van, I noticed the A-frame board that read 'Closed Tonight. Sorry' was still there, but I'm sure it was our fault the venue was empty that night.

Inexplicably, Colin didn't last long at that pub. I watched with interest and a morbid sense of glee as I saw his Facebook posts get more and more aggressive about the villagers until his final post a few months later was,

'Fuck the lot of you. I'm going to Ibiza.'

Bagpipes and Parental Expectations

For a while, myself and a friend were running a few open mic nights close to home. For the most part, it was a thoroughly heartwarming experience, with plenty of people popping their *Open Mic cherry* and throwing their hats into the ring. There's something really special about seeing up-and-coming performers taking their first steps in the wonderful world of entertainment. It makes me bubble with pride even if I've never met them before, and seeing performers coming back week in and week out and gaining confidence is a joy you won't find anywhere else.

There were, of course, a fair few divas, but we strived to make our open mic nights an all-inclusive night where the only thing that was frowned on was a huge ego. The worst performers of the night usually got the biggest cheer. The bagpipe player never tuned up before he was actually on stage. The pub invariably cleared before he got to start whatever song he was planning to play because, as you may or may not know, the sound of a bagpipe being 'readied' for performance is akin to an over-amplified goose laying an oversized egg. There were, of course, rather too many 'music to strangle cats to' moments, and at one open mic, a very, very, very drunk guy decided that this was the night he would try improv poetry. All in all, though, these events became the highlight of my week. I was giving back to them in the early stages of their career something I dearly wished I'd had when I'd started out.

My least favourite of these Open Mic events was the monthly one at the pub by the station that was well known for regular drug raids. There were also rumours that the landlord paid his staff in coke. It didn't surprise me at all, and I must say, I think he paid himself too much of it on some nights. Most months, we'd turn up and be greeted by the landlord looking sideways at us, with his glassy red eyes darting about all over the place. Invariably, he'd say the same thing every month when he saw us loading in,

'Oh, is that tonight?'

Mark was a proper London geezer. With a bold collection of gold chains and diamond-encrusted signet rings, his open shirt revealed a hairy chest, and the shape of his nostrils revealed that he should lay off the coke just a little.

We *could* have earned a fortune running the open mic at Mark's pub. Several times a night, he'd come up and speak to one of us, his bulging money clip in his hand, and ask if he'd paid us yet. On his most coked-up night, I counted eight times.

There were always some fun regulars at these events. First, there was Bill and Jen, an elderly couple who'd been together for some 60 years. Jen made me uncomfortable with how sexual she got with her guitar. She adored her guitar a little too much and would gyrate with it about the stage. At the same time, Bill stood to one side with his nipple-length white beard and hair, waiting for permission to take a quick flute solo before Jen retook control with her amorous advance to her poor instrument. I'd always have the same conversations with Bill and Jen - Bill would tell us at the end of the evening how much fun he'd had and how great the sound was, and Jen would complain that the sound was terrible and had ruined her performance.

Then there was Stuart. Stuart was an arrogant prick who had a great deal of growing up to do. At 18 years old, he was an exceptional guitarist, and he knew it. He knew he could wipe the floor with any of the other performers, and whilst I looked forward to hearing him play, I didn't look forward to him coming off stage. When he'd had his chance to show off, he would sit at the bar and launch into a great tirade about how terrible every other performer was. Sure, some of them were pretty ropey, but I was damned if I was going to let Stuart's toxic energy affect the encouraging atmosphere we fostered at these events. After a few weeks of loud sniping, I threw Stuart out, telling him he wasn't welcome until he fixed his attitude. Give him his due; he returned two years later and offered to play backing for anyone who wanted to perform. He was a delight. We lost touch, but I hope he's still got the same attitude.

A very nervous vocalist, Lucy, would come to open mic night dolled up to the nines and looking incredible. Just before getting up to perform, she'd change into her huge fluffy slippers so that if the stage fright got the better of her, she could close her eyes, scrunch her feet into her slippers and pretend she was practising at home. It worked, but it was a rather unique look!

At one bustling event with around 20 performers to fit in, a young kid turned up dressed in school uniform; guitar slung over his back, and mummy and daddy roadies carrying his amp and cables for him. He wanted to play an AC/DC song over a backing track, but when it came to his turn, he spent 15 minutes messing with the amp to get the right sound, tuning the guitar repeatedly, and generally faffing. I could see the other performers in the room getting impatient, so without allowing any more tinkering, I announced that he was ready to go and pressed go on the backing track. As the song started, I realised it was the live version of *Let There Be Rock* - an 11-minute track with a guitar riff that repeats over and over at the end. With control over the speaker system, I took the executive decision to fade him and the backing track out slowly after a reasonable number of repeated riffs. Sure, he and his family looked fit to burst, but it wasn't the 12-year-old Angus Young show - we had too many other performers to squeeze in.

As I was scooting around later in the evening, his mother grabbed me tightly by the arm and told me in no uncertain terms that she required a second performance for her son. She was rude, unpleasant and threatening, and I told her that her attitude was not conducive to our event. She left, shoving me into the door frame and loudly calling all the other performers in the room and me 'heathens'. Nice lady.

I never stuck to a specific order with the list of performers. Instead, I would wander around with my clipboard once I had the complete list of people on there and sit quietly with each person, asking them how they felt about their performance. Some wanted to get it out of the way immediately; others wanted a glass or two of wine before their slot. Some had such bad stage fright that I would allow them just to grab me and say, 'NOW,' if they felt ready, and the next person on the list would be temporarily bumped. It worked well. Rachel always needed three glasses of rosé, while Big Ron wanted to sing immediately so that he could curl up in the corner and nurse a few whiskeys.

Taylor was my favourite. A large, smiley guy who sweated just at the thought of being out in public, let alone performing. On his first occasion, he came into the pub just to have a look. He stayed the whole evening and left, saying he might play next time. The following week, he came but left his guitar in the car. The following week he came, brought the guitar in, left it behind the bar, and that's where it stayed. A week later, Taylor was back with his guitar, and this time, it sat at his feet all evening - not leaving the case. Just as I was starting to wonder if there was even anything in his case, he returned a week later with a guitar stand, and got the guitar out, left it on its stand... but still didn't play.

I will never forget the week Taylor played for the first time. He came into the bar, looking like a bunny in headlights. Ordering a triple vodka, he downed it in one, slammed the glass on the bar and said, 'Let's do it'. I escorted him to the stage, plugged his guitar in, introduced him and encouraged the audience to give him a round of applause. By this point, Taylor had been coming to open mic for probably a few months, so most people knew who he was. A deafening roar emanated from the audience, and Taylor's brow dripped visibly. Turning his back to the audience, he played for about three minutes. I can't even remember what the song was, but I remember his reaction once he finished. Turning to face the audience with a massive grin on his face, Taylor had well and truly overcome his stage fright.

'FUCK YEAH!' he screamed to an adoring crowd. I don' think he missed any of our open mic nights after that, and we ran them for at least 18 months.

One time, we were booked by a landlady who was new to the pub business. I don't think she knew what an open mic was. When we first arrived, she was angry at us because she'd seen that we were 'performing' at the pub down the road the next week, and she believed that it would affect the number of customers that would be in tonight if we spread ourselves too thinly. It turns out she thought my partner's stage name was *Open Mike*. She'd seen posters all over the local area for us and decided we were over-saturating the market. Turning people with guitars away at the door because we were having a private party didn't help much either, and when I came to the end of the evening to settle up with her, she asked how much *we* owed *her*. We only ran the open mic there once.

On one cold and wintery evening, we ran our one and only open mic night at a pub that smelled like perhaps they brought the cows into the bar overnight to get them out of the cold. There was an interesting collection of not-very-friendly faces sitting at the bar and a collection of terrified-looking people clutching guitars. One man was like the Venn diagram centre of these two groups. Gerry sat at the bar looking either drunk, ready to start a fight or both. Gerry was a rotund older gentleman who looked likely to be someone who sang sea shanties.

When it came to Gerry's turn to perform, my assumptions had been correct; he was indeed a folky singer-songwriter with a penchant for outrageously long sea shanties. The plan had been for each performer to be given the chance to showcase three songs, and then if there was time, there'd be a lightning round of one song each. Jerry took the piss. His first song lasted 8 minutes. Combine that with his ten-minute introduction; he was already eating into his allotted time and garnering glares from the other performers. He looked out at the audience whilst rambling about his entire life history, giving me the opportunity to smile at him and tap my watch. He nodded, apologised for waffling and immediately launched into American Pie. Once Gerry had finally finished this one, I hopped up to the mic and whispered in his ear that we'd have to call it two songs for him based on the time on the stage of his performance so far. He seemed affable enough and sloped off to the bar to top up his Guinness.

The evening went ok after that. I did notice that any time I stepped outside and came back in again the ageing cowpat smell was a touch overpowering, but everyone seemed pretty happy.

We'd set up by the pub's back door, so when the session was over, we could pile our gear out through these doors and straight into the van without having to climb through everyone. It seemed like a good idea until Gerry decided he'd like to entertain the remaining punters in the pub and plonked himself down right in the middle of all of our equipment. By this point, it was more than evident that he had had a significant number of whiskey chasers with his Guinness and was swaying somewhat unnervingly back and forth towards either speaker. Letting him know the evening was over and his services were no longer required didn't make any difference. Gerry was settled in for the night. That is until he leaned forward, completely face-planted himself on the floor, and began snoring. We spoke to the landlord as we cleared around Gerry and were told that takings from Gerry alone were the reason that they had remained in business for the past decade. It didn't surprise me.

Johnathan was a veteran open-mic performer. If there was an open mic within a 50-mile radius of his house, he was there. Most weeks, he attended 6 or 7 open mic nights and took the opportunity to perform every chance he could. Sometimes he came alone on his Harley, with his guitar strapped to his back; other times, he brought his long-suffering wife along. She sat quietly in the corner, sipping a lime and soda all evening. Johnathan was neither a good guitarist nor a good singer. It didn't matter. He was a charmingly happy performer whose long silver hair and pointy beard adorned a man who didn't take life too seriously. His guitar strums were in time with his voice, and if he forgot the words, he'd just add in a few extra strums. Everyone had learned not to join in with Johnathan - he marched to the beat of his own drum. Literally Johnathan's speciality was parody songs. I don't know where he found so many Weird Al-like lyric changes, but most weeks, he'd turn up with a new one prepared to plunge his audiences into fits of giggles. Imagine Bob Dylan half-singing-half-speaking through a Weird Al Yankovic song out of time. That was the Johnathan we all came to know and love.

The most heartbreaking open mic I ever ran involved a young woman called Tina. She was in her early twenties, with a slim figure and stunning blonde hair. I first became aware of her because her friend told me that Tina would like to perform but she didn't believe she could muster the confidence. I took a long time out of running around with my clipboard that night to talk to her, encourage her and generally see what I could do to convince her to perform. She told me she'd taken my comments on board and appreciated my time. She said she'd return the following week and see if she felt more confident.

The following week, there was Tina. She looked incredible. She was dressed in a figure-hugging black mini dress and stilettos with some classy pieces of vintage jewellery to top off the look. I knew the moment she came in the door that she planned to perform. She whisked me off, asking me to accompany her on the Peggy Lee song, Fever, and I happily agreed. I grabbed a guitar, and we even had a bit of a run-through in the loos for good measure.

Tina's voice was one of the best female vocals I have heard in person in all my time on the circuit. With a Randy Crawford-like voice that could melt the coldest of hearts, I was fighting back the tears by the time we'd run through her toilet-debut performance. I praised her highly and gave her all the encouragement I possibly could. As we went back into the main bar, she went to sit with her dad and wait for her turn to perform.

Tina stood up, ready to pop her open mic cherry. Shuffling to the stage, she looked like an A-lister who had just happened to be hanging out in the area and fancied a night off. Her stage presence and faked confidence carried her all the way to the microphone, at which point she announced that the audience should be kind to her because she was just '*having a go*' and hadn't done anything like this before. Cue colossal applause and I smiled at this beautiful community's support.

Tina was captivating. She'd have stolen the show if this had been a stadium gig and not just an open mic at the Queen's Head. Her performance was world-class. The nuances in her voice, the vibrato, everything about her performance screamed quality. At the end of the song, the audience erupted. This had been the performance of a lifetime with perfect pitch, poise and presence. Almost everyone was on their feet, screaming and applauding.

Almost everyone.

I noticed Tina's dad hadn't stood up and was scribbling furiously on a large piece of paper. I imagined perhaps he was writing a letter to her mother to tell her what a remarkable human their daughter was. I didn't really think anything of it.

Later on that evening, I found Tina in the loos. She was slumped on the floor, curled up in a ball. Her makeup was smudged, her previously lustrous and shiny hair matted and hanging over her face as she rocked back and forth sobbing.

I knelt beside her and cradled her in my arms until she slowly calmed down. Perhaps the response to her performance had overwhelmed her, and she wasn't sure how to handle it.

'In your own time,' I told her, hoping she'd confide in me.

Tina wept for a little longer until, eventually, she looked up at me and said,

'I'm just not good enough. I want this so much, but I'm just not good enough.'

I reminded her of the standing ovation, the whoops for more, and the smiles on everyone's faces. Nothing made any difference. Something had convinced Tina that all that was fake praise and that they weren't applauding out of delight; they were mock-applauding. According to Tina, it was a cruel joke that everyone in the pub had played on her that night.

'What on earth makes you think that, Tina?' I said as I reached out to wipe a tear from her face. I knew this community of musicians inside out, and I was damn sure that their response was completely genuine.

'Dad made some notes on my performance,' she said, eventually.

'He said I was the laughing stock of the evening and tha I'd embarrassed him.'

Anger bubbled up inside me to boiling point. I've seen so many musicians lose their way because of a snide remark from a parent or partner, and I wasn't going to let this world-class singer feel this way any longer. Not on my watch.

I stormed out of the ladies' and approached her dad. In front of him on the table were two A4 sheets of paper with small messy handwriting on both sides. I picked one up and started reading it.

The word 'love' was slightly sharp', 'never - too whiney', 'Fever - overly dramatic - sounded like Miss Piggy'. The list went on and on and on.

I grabbed Tina's dad's two pages of hatred from the table and marched up to the microphone. Standing there, tearing each page into little tiny pieces in front of Tina, her dad and all of the performers felt like the right thing to do.

'There is no room for this kind of attitude at our open mic nights,' I said. Most people in the room didn't know what I was talking about, but they could see the earnestness in my face, so they all began applauding.

I walked off the stage and returned to Tina's table. I have a special word for people who behave like this towards their children. I called him it. Loudly. Then I said he should leave.

Tina and I are still friends. She is estranged from her father and has been utterly nailing a significant role in London's West End for the past few months. I couldn't be prouder.

A rookie wedding planner and a hungry band

We pulled into the car park, checked the time, and congratulated ourselves that, despite having used the M25, we had still managed to get to the venue 5 minutes early. There's a knack to planning your arrival if you've used the M25: estimate 45mph and add two hours. That way, you can guarantee 95% of the time that you will arrive early or bang on time, no matter what the GPS tells you.

The M25 gods had been good to us that day, which was a good thing seeing as we were playing at a wedding reception. From our conversations with Judy, the wedding planner, meticulous time management was a quality she expected from us. One which she had consistently reminded us about in the weeks leading up to the wedding. Over the course of the month, we'd received emails with headers such as, 'Just a gentle reminder...' and 'Please don't forget...' and my personal favourite, 'Please make sure to be on time or you won't get paid.'

Arriving at 1:55 p.m. for our 2 p.m. deadline made us all feel just a touch smug. Judy had made it abundantly clear she had a very low opinion of musicians and our knowledge of punctuality, so this was a win for us as far as we were concerned.

I quickly popped into the building to find out the lay of the land. A woman with a clipboard made a beeline for me, and as she walked towards me, I reached out my hand, smiled and said, 'You must be Judy.'

Judy was a young woman, perhaps very early 20s, and sporting high heels and a pinstripe navy business suit jacket and trousers to match. Under her jacket was a white chiffon blouse with a gold brooch covering the top button. Her hair was neatly tied in a perfect bun atop her head, with eyebrows plucked to within an inch of their life. She was immaculate. Not wedding-guest immaculate. City-businesswoman immaculate. It didn't sit right for a July wedding.

'Well, who are you then?' she enquired in possibly the most officious tone I've ever heard. I told her my name, and midway through telling her my reason for being there, she interrupted me,

'Why are you here already?'

'Because your email said to be here no later than 2 p.m.' I double-checked my watch for clarity as I spoke.

Judy looked visibly agitated,

'I don't want you here yet; you shouldn't be here yet.' I frowned, went back to the van to grab the paperwork and returned with it, pointing to the section in bold caps lock that said, '*BE HERE FOR NO LATER THAN 2 P.M.*'

'Musicians are always late,' she replied with a sweeping gesture to go with the insulting stereotyped verbal sweep. 'You'll have to sit in the car park.'

Picking my jaw up from the floor, I turned to head back to the van and tell the rest of the band about my encounter. As I walked through the main doors, Judy yelled after me, '... and don't come back in until I say so.'

We sat in the van for at least two hours until my bladder ran out of patience, and I went back to the venue searching for a loo. Judy was barking orders at the professional photographer and complaining that he hadn't brought any throwaway cameras for the guests. I caught his eye as it was mid-roll. Seemingly, her professional stereotype of his chosen career hadn't sat well with him either. He grinned at me, later telling me that it was her first wedding planner gig and she hadn't appreciated him telling her that it wasn't his 'first rodeo.'

Judy glared at me,

'What are you doing back in here?' She tutted when I told her I'd come in search of a loo. She huffed and sneered when I said to her that it'd be nice to know when we could eat as well because, after a long journey and two hours of sitting in a hot, stuffy van, we were all starting to get a little peckish.

'We're not serving food for the staff,' she said matter-of-factly. We were now also on *red alert,* apparently, and not to leave the premises because, at any point, she may summon us to perform with a click of her impeccably preened fingernails.

I'd had enough.

'So, just to clarify, you want the 6 of us to arrive at 2 and sit in our van until you require us, we're unlikely to leave the venue before midnight, and you're not going to provide any food, despite our agreement saying that you will?'

I caught the photographer fake-applauding me out over her shoulder. Thankfully one of the kitchen staff overheard the conversation and told me they had tons of food left over. He promised to plate us up some meals and gestured to a table marked 'band' as Judy sneered into her clipboard again.

While we sat at the 'band' table enjoying our food, Judy came over to ask how long it would take us to get set up. It's a six-piece band plus engineer, and by the time we've loaded everything onto the stage and sound-checked every instrument, run through a song or two to make sure everything sounds okay, it usually takes about two hours. Judy was not happy with this information. It was 7 p.m., and we were expected to start playing at 9 p.m. on the dot.

'But, you can't set up yet; there's still the speeches to do. Not to mention there are diners on the stage still eating their desserts.' I could see Judy was getting twitchy.

'You can start playing after the speeches,' she said as she spun on her pointy little stiletto and bustled away.

There was nothing else to do but sit at our table and listen to the speeches. Judy's instructions were clear: we must not bring a single thing in from the van until she said so. Finally, at around 9:15 p.m., the speeches drew to a natural conclusion, and Judy stepped onto the stage, clapping her hands together for attention.

'And now.... the band,' Judy smiled at the audience and gestured to our table, leading the applause.

Out of respect for the bride and groom, our sound engineer hooked up a speaker and played recorded music within about ten minutes. We managed to get set up quickly and started playing about an hour later. According to a conversation with the bride's mother, as we were packing away at 2 a.m., it was to be Judy's first and last 'gig' as a wedding planner.

Drums and trombones

What exactly are you supposed to say to an audience member who clambers past the sign that says *No audience members past this point, please,* up onto the stage, stands right next to the drummer and asks,

'So, how do you get those drum sounds?'

This is what we were faced with at the end of what was otherwise a cracking gig in North Yorkshire. I've heard some doozies before, but this one was a whole new level of what-the-fuck. We all turned and stared at her, waiting to see if the cogs would jam themselves into place and the lady would promptly apologise for what we all assumed was a fleeting moment of muppetry.

But no. After we all stared at her for longer than was comfortable for any of us, she continued,

'Is it some sort of electronic trigger or something?'

'No,' loooooooooong pause, 'it's an acoustic drum kit.' Bewildered expressions all around.

'Yes, but how do you get that low thumpy thump noise and the ting-te-ting noises?' The poor woman looked absolutely flummoxed.

The only way to explain how a drum kit works was for our guy to sit behind it and play it. 'Right foot, see, thump thump,' he said as he pointed to the beater pedal. 'Left foot, ting ting,' pointing again to the hi-hat pedal. Then, picking up his sticks, he hit the snare, toms, and cymbals. 'Like this,' he smiled. 'Does that make sense?'

'But how do you know which sound you're going to get?' Our new friend still looked baffled. 'Where does it plug in?'

The only thing to do was to usher her carefully off the stage, informing her that we had a curfew and had to get packed away now. As she stepped off the stage, she looked me straight in the eye and said,

'I've never heard a trombone played like that before.' It made me so glad I'd spent 5 minutes explaining what a soprano saxophone is to what I'd thought was an attentive audience.

Speaking with the promoter at the end of the night, he remarked on how we'd all seemed to have been having a lovely chat with Iris. Apparently, Iris attends every single gig at this venue without fail. If he hadn't told us that, we'd have been convinced that she'd never before seen (or heard) anyone making music.

A miserable Yorkshireman and a pixie with an attitude

'I ain't movin',' said the overweight Yorkshireman as he folded his arms and glared at me as if I was the sole reason for every problem he'd ever had in his miserable little life.

I'd somehow found myself in a pub, miles from home, in a stand-off (or, more accurately, a sit-off) with a total stranger. He seemed pretty adamant and clutched his Guinness as if his life depended on it. But, on the other hand, I was simply trying to do what the barmaid had asked me to do, so I wasn't sure what the reason for all the aggression was.

I'd arrived in the village ten minutes earlier, having struggled to find this tiny remote pub in the middle of almost nowhere. It was a Monday night, and it really wasn't shaping up to be a very promising evening.

Josie, the barmaid, was a sweet little elfish-looking girl with a cheeky grin and feather earrings that looked handmade. She had an air about her that said *don't mess with me,* even though she looked no more than about 100 pounds. From the encounters I'd had so far with the gentleman in the corner, I could see she was the perfect person to be in charge of the pub.

Realising my discussions were going nowhere with the charmer in the corner, I turned back to Josie to see if she had any resolutions. She'd asked me to move the gentleman and his table so I could set up to perform in 'his' corner. Logistically, she'd said, it was the best spot in the pub for me to stand because I wouldn't be disturbed by people to-ing and fro-ing to the toilets, the front door, or the kitchen door. It made perfect sense to me.

Not to the comfortable guy, however. Nope. He 'ain't movin'.' That was that. Josie grinned her cheeky grin, and I just knew she was about to work some magic.

Josie cleared her throat loudly in a mock attention-grabbing style,

'Haa hmmmm, folks, Brian is being a dick again, so if you want to hear live music tonight, I'm going to need each and every one of you to pick up your meals and your tables and shuffle everything around until Mr Fussy-Pants is happy.'

Everyone in the bar either laughed heartily or groaned, 'OH BRIAN, not again.'

Josie continued,

'If anyone loses any of their fish, chips and mushy peas in the process of reshuffling, you have my permission to steal Brian's food.'

I think we all loved Josie that night.

Once every other table had dutifully shuffled around, I set up in my new spot, smiling and making friends with the customers in the pub. Admittedly, this was mainly through a shared loathing of my new mortal enemy, Brian, who was sneering over his pint, possibly trying to place some kind of hex on me.

The gig was a whole lot of fun. I had a genuinely captive audience, and the atmosphere in that tiny Yorkshire pub was positively electric that night. Smiles, warm applause, laughter at my stories and a general camaraderie made me feel on top o the world.

The audience roared with laughter as I sang *'Clowns to the left of me,'* and pointed at Brian, who was seething so much I thought he might have a Mr Creosote moment and explode ir front of us all. It would have been annoying if he did because everyone would probably have to move their dinners out of the way, and Brian had already been the centre of attention for quite long enough that evening.

The audience's dislike of Brian was evident, and not jus for his *fussy-pants* moment this evening. There was clearly a long-term animosity between Brian and the people of this tiny village. You could almost feel sorry for him if it wasn't for the obnoxious heckling and his stoic approach to being far less welcome than me. And I was only there for the night.

Halfway through my second set, I knew I had developec a relationship with the audience where I couldn't put a foot wrong. The type of relationship that every musician strives for It was at this point that I decided to try something. Brian had left his *special spot* to top up his Guinness and visit the loo. Sc stepping away from the stage area, I decided I was going to go and sit in Brian's chair. A brave move perhaps, given that

Brian had been decidedly disagreeable all evening, but I knew I had the audience on my side, and more than anything, I knew that tough-as-nails Josie would step in if needed. So, I took Brian's freshly poured Guinness from the bar and shot Josie the same cheeky grin she'd shot me earlier. I wandered over and slumped into Brian's chair, folding my arms across my chest.

I was right. The audience was indeed 100% on my side. A little ripple of giggles had developed into full-blown howls by the time Brian returned from the loo. Brian's face was a picture. Sober enough to realise how unchivalrous it would have been to expel me unceremoniously from his seat in front of an audience who were clearly on my side, he stood motionless, his face redder and redder with no idea what to do. Finally, after our second mini sit-off of the night, I stood up and returned to the stage area. Brian nestled back in his spot, muttering.

The audience seemed disappointed and started calling out for something else to happen. Neither they nor I knew what that something was, but they all began shouting 'Sarah, Sarah, Sarah,' like a slow football chant. Then, confident that I had the audience on my side, I returned to Brian and sat in his lap.

That. That was his line.
I returned to the stage covered in Guinness, and Brian hurriedly left the pub. So much of a hurry that we heard his tyres squealing up the road as I performed my next song. Choosing to play a few Irish tunes to match the smell of Guinness on my clothes, I somehow managed to win the audience just a little more.

I spent a long time at the bar after the gig chatting with Josie. She told me it was a privately owned pub without any ties to any breweries, which on the one hand, meant they could choose which beers they had on tap and make plenty of their own decisions about how to manage the pub and what to put on the menu. But, sadly, it also meant that without a safety net, they had to endure Brian. Josie told me Brian's tab made up about a third of the pub's weekly income, and much as everyone utterly despised him, he was the sole reason the pub remained open. It's closed now, which is a shame. I can only imagine Brian died of alcohol poisoning or, more likely, a lynch mob and the pub couldn't keep going without him.

As I sat talking to Josie, I realised how comfortable we felt in each other's company. It had been a truly memorable night, and we'd really bonded. I admired her confidence and her unique sense of style. With her feather earrings and pixie haircut, she carried herself with a real 'I-don't-care-if-you-like-me' attitude, making her even more likeable. As a creative type, it's hard trying not to care if people like you or not. We put ourselves and our craft out there for all to see, and we all desperately want to be liked. Josie was inspiring.

I remarked on how cool her outfit was: a figure-hugging denim dungarees-like dress that would make a fantastic stage outfit.

'I think it'd suit you,' she smiled and promptly took it off and handed it to me.

Mud sandwiches and tantrums

We'd been put forward for the prestigious opportunity to open for a guy who was a total dick. Everyone on the circuit knew he was a total dick, and the consensus from anyone who had met him was that... you guessed it... yes, he's a total dick. For some reason, the guy has quotes on his website describing him as a 'kind and endearing performer' who 'always has time for his audiences' and 'gives a spectacular show.' Having seen his show and his attitude to his audiences and fellow musicians, I'd like to call bullshit. This is Emperor's New Clothes syndrome.

I didn't think opening for the guy (let's call him the Emperor) would further our career, but people around us, especially the guy who put us forward, said that it would be the making of us.

I looked up the venue's name on Google and found it to be a huge, almost arena-sized place. There were photos of big household names playing there, with what looked like a fantastic stage and spectacular light show. Fair enough, we were in. I called back with a definite 'yes.'

Leading up to the gig, our band did the usual *talk-about-it-on-social-media-as-much-as-possible* thing and tried to build some hype for the gig. Unfortunately, every time we tagged the Emperor in a Facebook update, he almost instantly removed it. Any talk of the gig on his social media made no mention of a support act, and the photos we'd sent for publicity to his promoter were nowhere to be seen. I hoped things would pick up once we got closer to the time.

We hopped in our little gig-mobile and headed off up the M1. Arriving early at the venue, we sneaked in the side door to find the lighting rig being set up. Holy crap, it was sensational! We decided to disappear and find somewhere to have coffee to kill time. We were not nervous, but the adrenaline was flying around that little coffee shop. After an hour or so of psyching ourselves up and 'what ifs' and 'maybes' conversations, we returned to the venue where we met Alice, the Emperor's manager/publicist/booking agent/promoter/

sound engineer/ girlfriend/general dogsbody, who had just pulled up in her hearing-aid-coloured Fiat Uno.

It was a little worrying that we had to tell her twice who we were. We'd conversed a fair bit, and, of course, she had all our publicity photos... didn't she?

Alice offered to show us the venue and the green room. Wanting not to appear too excited, we kept quiet that we'd already poked our heads around the door. She elbowed open the doors, and we followed her in.

The light show set up was in full flow now, and every colour of the rainbow was bouncing and flashing and swirling around the room, making it hard to see where Alice was headed. Walking diagonally across the room, Alice held open a door on the other side. We followed her into some kind of office area with printers buzzing and whirring and telephones ringing from all directions.

Alice introduced us to a bunch of people whose names I forgot immediately and then led us through another door into a small room with black paint on the walls and ceiling, a bar in one corner and about twenty chairs facing a small makeshift stage.

'Are you nervous?' Alice asked. 'We're almost sold out.'

'In fact,' she said, gesturing around the room, 'we may have to put a few more chairs out.'

My heart sank. This. This was the colossal gig that we'd driven hours to get to. This was the massive opportunity that we'd been talking about all over social media. This was the career-changing moment we'd been psyching ourselves up about whilst overdosing on coffee half an hour earlier.

With that, Alice scuttled off back to her Fiat Uno to grab her sound system so that she could set it up for us to soundcheck.

Oh.

Meanwhile, one of the people we'd been introduced to offered to show us to the green room where we were to meet the Emperor.

When we arrived at the green room, I decided to make the best of a bad situation. We'd been warned about the Emperor's short temper, but I was damned if I would see the evening get any worse. I gave him my biggest, broadest smile and reached out my hand,

'Hi, I'm Sarah. Nice to meet you.'

The Emperor neither shook my hand nor adjusted his gaze. In the most disdainful tone I think I had ever heard (even worse than the one my mother used when I told her I wanted to be a professional musician), he muttered from the corner of his mouth,

'Yes. I know who you are. Don't touch anything in the fridge, and don't touch my wine.'

With that, he somehow managed to sit astride every single chair in the green room and started restringing his guitar, leaving little bits of the metal guitar strings poked deliberately into the sofa cushions, maybe to make his point or something. The rumours were correct! I was indeed dealing with a total dick!

Alice, by this point, had set up her suitcase PA. It was like a *Fisher Price* speaker system that tottered on either side of the already precarious makeshift stage.

Calling that she was ready for us to soundcheck, she asked whether we'd enjoyed the meal she'd laid out for us in the green room.

'Oh... was that meant for us?' I asked with a slight smirk. '*Perhaps you should teach the other people in the green room how to share,*' I thought.

Continuing his theme of being unable to share, the Emperor pulled a chair onto the stage while we were setting up. Right here was where he'd decided he wanted to tune his guitar. All the way through our sound-check, '*twang, twang TWANG TWANNNNGGGGGG*' rang out. I could see Alice was frustrated too, twiddling with knobs on her *Fisher Price* sound system until I asked her whether it wouldn't be better if we sound-checked after the Emperor had finished whatever it was that he was trying to achieve.

'I'm the fucking star,' said the Emperor, spinning around in his incredibly tacky, fake snakeskin boots.

'You're the fucking support act. Why don't you know your fucking place?'

I wish I was embellishing to make the story more interesting. I'm not even paraphrasing. I scribbled it word for word in my notebook, which I carry everywhere because I just knew I'd need it one day. I hope you appreciate the effort here - he saw me doing it!

Now the Emperor's hissy fit was reaching epic proportions. Throwing down his cliché cowboy hat at my feet, he stropped back to the green room. I assume to eat the rest of my dinner.

We had a quick band meeting. Nowhere had it been advertised that we were playing there, we weren't being paid (because we'd earned the 'privilege' to support the Emperor), and we were hungry, tired and fed up. So we did what any self-respecting musician does. We pulled out all the stops for the audience. They paid a ticket price, and even though they weren't there to see us, they weren't there to see us go through the motions either. So we gave it our everything. All 16 (yes, 16 - Alice had to take some chairs away in the end so that she could describe the event as *SOLD OUT* on social media the next day) people in the audience were on their feet at the end of our set, cheering for more with the volume and energy that we'd been expecting when we'd first walked into the venue that afternoon.

I jumped off the stage at the end of our set, grinning inanely, and sat on the side of it with a box of CDs. The audience formed a reasonably orderly queue, and I honestly think we won every one of them. There were smiles and hugs all around.

Judging by the queue, I was about halfway through selling CDs when the Emperor came up, picked up the box of CDs and thrust it into my lap, closing it as he did so.

'Thissssssss. Is. Not. Your. Gig.' Ah, the hissy fit wasn't over.

'Fuck it,' I thought. There's no winning this guy over. There's no reasoning with him. Perhaps he's suffering from crippling stage fright, and he'll be a lovely guy once he's played to these 16 people. Either way, his issues were not mine, and the rest of the band and I decided to retire quietly to the back of the room.

The room quietened. The Emperor staggered onto the stage and opened his mouth to address his audience,

'What the fuck happened to my career to mean I have to play in this shit hole?'

Who says that? Who treats an audience like that? Who behaves like that? What is up with this guy? I've always thought that no matter where you are in your career, you're there because of the fans. You are nothing without them. It's why the likes of Bob Dylan annoy me. The idea that you can treat your fans like this is abhorrent. They're the reason you have a job.

Seemingly, it was abhorrent to a few audience members, too, who loudly declared their (now) mutual disdain for the Emperor. By the time the first song started, there were 12 people in the audience, plus us, the bar staff, and Alice. We sneaked out the back after a few more songs, returning to the green room in search of our bags and something to eat while the rabid, spoilt guard dog couldn't defend his territory.

The scene in the green room cemented our opinion of the Emperor. Three empty red wine bottles sat on the counter. Every single sandwich from a giant platter had one bite taken out of it. Our bags and coats had been removed from the hangers and thrown on the floor, covered in muddy footprints. The Emperor was not the charming, endearing consummate professional, his website claims. Not by a long way.

We used the money from the CD sales to pay for the gas home. We even squeezed a couple of petrol station sandwiches out of it too. The following morning we had 16 new fans on our Facebook page.

Silver linings.

Not an interesting story

I feel, for the sake of balance, that I should write about a great gig that I played once back in those days that had no hitches, the promoter didn't screw us over the fee, it was well advertised with posters all over town and lots of social media updates from them about how and where to buy tickets. The promoter was kind and cheerful to us all evening. We were thrilled to be there, and they were delighted to have us. The event was sold out, and we were rebooked on the spot.

Not the most exciting story, is it? And that's why, despite the fantastic promoters and excellent gigs I've played, I'm here ... telling you about the other ones.

Now, back to normal...

A dayglo tent and an ego problem

I could have had an orgy in my dayglo orange tent jacket, and no one would have noticed.

'We only have five XL size high-vis jackets left,' the festival organiser, Tracey, told me as I'd slipped my arm into one side of my fat-builder-chic outfit for the day. I looked like a traffic cone.

I'd been up since 5 a.m., loading the van with just about every single piece of sound equipment I had. Along with my drum kit, mic stands, mics, cables, and music stands, the van was heaving under the weight of it all as I plodded along the A272 to Billingshurst, where I'd volunteered to run sound for one of the stages at a festival. I'd been given the *originals band* stage to look after, and as the day began to drag on, I started to wonder if I would meet anyone that day who *didn't* think they were the Next Big Thing.

Some of the acts were, to their credit, well-rehearsed and creative. They pulled a crowd as the Saturday afternoon shoppers went about their business. A duo further down the high street outside Sainsbury's stopped everyone in their tracks as they blasted out a rollicking version of *Brown Sugar*. I strained to listen to them as I tried to zone out the latest blue-haired punk band on the stage I was managing.

Each band was given 30 minutes to an hour to perform, and it was a quick change around between acts. Unfortunately, there was no allowance for me to take a break, so I had to rely on the honesty and kindness of passers-by every time I needed a wee. I returned each time, hoping the volunteer I'd left staffing the desk wasn't someone who had tinkered with the settings. By lunchtime, my stomach was growling louder than the shouty rock band baring their teenage angst to anyone who'd listen.

Right on time, Tracey arrived with hot dogs, burgers, tomato soup and several cups of tea for me. She hugged me tightly and thanked me for volunteering, pausing only to smirk at my orange tent outfit before skipping off to serve the next weary stage manager.

Fully refuelled and feeling significantly less *hangry*, I ushered the next band onto the stage. I'd guess the average of the band to be perhaps 17. All five guys were dressed from head to toe in black, with dyed black hair and chains hanging from anything it was possible to hang chains from. They were the picture of happiness, calling themselves Satan's Moodswingers... or something like that.

I ran a quick soundcheck with them and adjusted a few things on the desk. The vocalist stepped up to the mic and very quietly said,

'Check one-two. Yeah, it's working.'

'*I know it's working. It's been working all day, you dear little cloud of misery,*' I thought.

'Can you give me a couple of lines of the volume you expect to sing at, please?' I asked certain his whisper wasn't his singing volume.

Mr. Doom and Gloom tutted at me, sighed and repeated, just as quietly,

'check one, two, check check.'

Clearly, this was their first-ever soundcheck. Maybe nerves had gotten the better of them. I shook my head and left them to it.

I gave them the thumbs up to get started, knowing I'd have to adjust as I went along. The band started up, and they were tight and impressive. I adjusted a few knobs and made the kick drum really thump through the speakers. This was heavy and intricate metal.

...And then the vocalist came in.

'DEAAAAAAAAAAAAAAAAAAAAAAAAATHHHHHHHH!' he screeched at the top of his voice, causing me, my speakers, and the whole of Billingshurst to wince. I lurched at the dials and quickly made adjustments. Normality resumed.

As I stood there, reacting as quickly as I could to each new situation, I noticed that aside from myself, there were five middle-aged men, arms folded, watching the band. I soon realised these were the dads of the band - each nodding slightly out of time and doing their best to look as if they were enjoying themselves.

One of them approached me and told me he was the drummer's dad.

'Best they've ever sounded,' he said, shaking my hand.

Distracted temporarily from the stage, I looked back to notice in horror that the lead vocalist was jumping up and down on my stage monitors, kicking his feet into the mesh grill each time he jumped off. *I don't think so, mister!*

Muting him between songs, I walked up to the stage and (fairly politely) let him know this wasn't acceptable.

'That's just my stage presence, luv. It's how I roll,' he yelled as if he thought he was Liam Gallagher.

'Not with my equipment, you don't,' I smiled as he tried to continue singing into his muted mic.

The scrawny little charmer turned his back on me and gestured a finger across his throat to the rest of the band. They stopped.

'Fackin' bitch turned my mic off,' he screamed for all the dads to hear. *They must be so proud*, I thought. I muted him again,

'Don't you know who I am?' I smiled as the tantrumming rock star wannabe jumped up and down, stamping his feet on the stage.

'No,' he sulked, 'who the fuck do you think you are? Someone special?'

'I'm the person that volunteered to get up at 5 a.m. to load my van, drive here, set up all of my equipment, and manage fuckwits like you all day long.'

Give him his due, he calmed down, semi-apologised, and they finished their set without issue. As they were packing away, one of the other dads came to speak to me,

'That was the worst I've ever heard them. The sound was shit, thanks to you. They're bigger than this kind of bollocks.'

'I'm gonna go ahead and guess you're the vocalist's dad,' I smiled widely at him.

'I am,' he said, 'how did you know?'

Stage fright and nits

I was in an all-girl band for an extremely brief period in my early career. We rehearsed for about six months, did one gig and then called it a day thanks to the singer's crippling stage fright. As a result, we didn't even come up with a band name, although '*Flaps*' was a distasteful but strong contender.

I had responded to an advert in the local newspaper seeking female musicians to take over the world. It was around the time the Spice Girls were huge, and every single female musician had decided that the early 2000s was their time.

I went along to the audition at a rather dodgy-looking rehearsal studio in a back alley on the outskirts of Brighton. I was greeted by Deb (who placed the advert), Lea, Annette, Zola and Mickey on arrival.

Mickey confused me. The advert was for an all-girl band, and I couldn't tell what was going on with them at all. The voice, name and chest hair suggested that perhaps Mickey was male. On the other hand, the sundress and heavy makeup suggested otherwise. But hey, it was Brighton, and anything goes in Brighton.

It wasn't long before I realised what Deb had meant when she'd placed an advert for an all-girl band. It wasn't so much about putting a band together as seeking like-minded lesbians for a bit of fun on a Tuesday night. Deb was married with three children. She was around 6 feet tall and butch looking, with a startlingly large collection of dungarees and a haircut that said, '*Can I please speak to the manager*'.

Deb had some issues with her sexuality and swayed violently between 'full-time mum with an oblivious husband' and 'promiscuous homosexual that frequents the gay bars of Brighton any night her husband is home to look after the kids'. It must have been hell for her, and she wrestled with her lifestyle. Most of the time, she took out her frustrations on us: frequently stopping a song to yell about a mistake or, more regularly, yelling at us if she'd made a mistake. Her perfectionism was clearly aimed at disguising her inner turmoil. We could all see through it and didn't raise it with her. She had enough to deal with.

Lea was an interesting character. A hippy through and through, with wild black and grey hair covering a beautiful face. Her bottom lip always had a joint stuck to it. Lea wore black from head to toe and smelled like a combination of weed and patchouli. I liked her instantly. She was more welcoming than Deb, who came across as a little Sergeant Major-ish. Lea was a true animal lover. Vegan and obsessed with fixing the world one cow eater at a time. She was so obsessed that when she got nits from a child she'd been babysitting, she refused to use nit shampoo because, in her mind, the poor little creatures had just as much right to live as she did.

Annette was a talented musician. She could pick up a bass or guitar and play absolutely anything. I learned after a few rehearsals that she was also a superb drummer, but Lea wanted to be the drummer, so Annette wasn't allowed. Annette had a giant smiley face, a boyish haircut and more plaid shirts than all the Canadian woodsmen combined probably own.

Zola, bless Zola. Zola had very recently come out and was struggling with it. Although she wasn't entirely sure if she was gay, she just thought Deb seemed to be having a great time and thought she'd 'like to give the whole thing a whirl,' as she said. Her parents had disowned her on account of Zola no longer meeting their supposedly Christian values, and she was struggling with trying to find a look that said both *'Fuck You'* and also *'Please be kind; I'm a little fragile.'* Most weeks, Zola came to rehearsals trying out a brand new look. Once, it was a cutesie pastel blue polka dot dress with heavy black eye makeup. Another time, she arrived dressed head to toe in leather but with her hair in side bunches framed with baby pink ribbons. I must admit to a slightly raised eyebrow when she turned up in a full-size red and white *Cat In The Hat* hat. Zola was reinventing herself every week but was too fragile to ask any of us what we thought of each new look. Instead, she scanned the room for hints of disdain or upturned noses and adjusted her look the following week, depending on her perceived level of contempt from each of us. Zola was struggling with every aspect of her existence, and if it weren't for Deb's wandering hands and Lea's nits, I'd have suggested a group hug on more than one occasion.

We rehearsed for around six months. I say '*rehearsed*' when I really mean that we spent two hours in a rehearsal room tinkering about, followed by a further 3 or 4 in the pub. During one of these pub meetings early on, Deb compared us to the Spice Girls. During that same pub session, I also discovered the girls had assumed I was gay too, simply because I'd answered an ad from an all-female band in Brighton. Nope!

I came up with Spice Girl-Esque nicknames for all of us that I didn't dare share with them: Butch Spice, Curious Spice, Hippy Spice, Boy (?) Spice, Married Spice and me: Straight Spice.

After six months of rehearsing and drinking, Zola got us a gig. At that point, we hadn't even got a name, and the rehearsing was starting to wear a bit thin for me. I was working with a couple of other bands that were keeping me busy, and I was beginning to feel that this wasn't going anywhere. Still, Zola had got us a fairly respectable booking at an excellent venue on Brighton seafront, so we zipped through the nine songs we'd managed to work on during our rehearsal-pub sessions and decided we were ready.

It was awful. Zola displayed the most paralysing stage fright that I've ever seen in anyone. Standing up to the mic, she clutched her water bottle and sang without moving a muscle. Annette and Mickey both decided they wanted to be the bassist that night, and Lea also made it very clear she didn't want to be a drummer anymore if she wasn't allowed to stop mid-song to tickle her nits with her drumsticks. Deb and I held it together as best we could, but it was a shit show.

It was my first and last gig with that band. We'd rehearsed for six months, come up with nine cover songs that we could muddle our way through, and we hadn't even decided upon a band name for the one gig we'd butchered. Still, there was plenty of booze, and Lea smoked enough weed to make us seem like the stereotypical band. We did not, unsurprisingly, take over the world as the Spice Girls did.

Too many dolls and an uninvited backing vocalist

Standing in a room full of immaculately dressed porcelain dolls, many of whom had eyes missing, I wondered how many other musicians there were in the world who had been paid in cash, cheese and deep tissue massages that night.

It had started out OK. I'd been booked to play at a small venue in Northeast Holland, close to the German border. I'd spent the morning pootling along in my little van and enjoying the terrified looks from drivers whenever they didn't realise quite quickly enough that they'd pulled alongside a right-hand drive car at the lights. The morning drive afforded me a relaxing afternoon walking along a beautifully serene and isolated coastal path and set me in the right frame of mind for an evening's gig.

On arrival, I was greeted by my hosts, Jan and Maria, an older couple who still had quite the twinkle in their eyes for each other. They welcomed me with open arms before leaving me to set up my gear on the stage. Jan bustled around placing tea lights on tables, trying to set the mood for the evening, while Maria scampered off to the kitchen and started rattling pots and pans and making the room smell delightful. I looked forward to whatever she had been concocting to be soon sitting comfortably in my belly.

Once I was set up, Jan, Maria, and I sat down to eat together. I'd read that Dutch food was '*more economical and filling than pleasing,*' so I'd prepared myself for a simple *meat and two veg* style dinner despite the intoxicating smells wafting up my nose.

Maria had excelled herself. There were many different types of sausages, some rye bread, a few not-so-exciting-looking overcooked vegetables and an absolute mountain of different types of cheese. The bread was tough and dense (which I later learned is typical for the region), and managed to stick to every tooth in my mouth. I made a mental note to ensure I cleaned my microphone before the next gig and tucked into the feast heartily.

Thanking Maria for the meal, I retired to the sofa, hoping that at least some of the food would settle before the gig started.

As the audience shuffled in, Jan and Maria mingled among them, making everyone feel warm and welcome. They were the perfect hosts in every way. As the evening went on, I noticed from the stage that no glass ever reached empty before being whisked away and replenished with military efficiency.

I sang a mixture of covers and originals that evening. Having spent quite a decent amount of time setting up the sound system, I was alarmed that, during some songs, a strange warbling sound emanated from somewhere. I couldn't quite figure out what it was, and after a few songs, I turned back to the mixer desk, apologising to the audience and tried to find the issue. Nothing was obvious, so I turned back to the audience and continued. Again, with the strange whining noise. I noticed it was only when I was singing, so I worried for a while that perhaps I'd deposited a little too much of that delicious rye bread into the mic, and maybe it was somehow creating an extra sound. Speaking to the audience without the mic, I quickly took it apart, shook it, and continued. Still strange noises. It was as if somewhere, perhaps just to my left, someone was slowly strangling a cat.

Eventually, I realised the sound was coming from a member of the audience. For whatever reason, one gentleman had decided that he knew all the songs in my set list (he didn't) and was adding in his own 'harmony' whenever the mood took him. Slowly, I snuck the speakers' volume up between the following few songs in the hope of drowning him out. Eventually, I reached a comfortable point between making him less prominent and making me too prominent and upsetting the audience at the front. I was happy and began to relax a little more into the evening.

It was an enjoyable gig, apart from my uninvited 'harmoniser.' Afterwards, I sat for quite some time into the evening with Jan and Maria, sampling a traditional local drink Beerenburg, a kind of herbal liquor, I think. Very odd, but the company was good, and the smiles were broad.

Maria brought out a gigantic tray of cheeses, pastries, and more rye bread from the kitchen, and we chatted into the evening. After a while, I couldn't stifle my yawns any longer and let out a spontaneously cavernous yawn which probably displayed more semi-digested rye bread than is socially acceptable. Maria offered to show me to my room and suggested that she give me a massage before I turned in. She was at pains to point out that she was a qualified masseuse, and this wasn't just a whole new turn in the evening's events.

'That sounds lovely,' I chirped, realising how much the long drive, the long walk and the gig had left me feeling a little stiff. Maria led me upstairs to her treatment room. Hundreds of old black and white photos of the surrounding area adorned the flock wallpaper in the hallway. It almost felt as though I was stepping back in time.

Maria worked out decades-worth of knots in my shoulders. I'd visit her every week if it weren't such a long drive. She was a master de-knotter and popped every last one of the niggles that I'd not even realised was there until they left my body with a satisfying clunk.

Standing up from Maria's table, I felt like I was walking after taking off a giant backpack. I felt as light as a feather and more chilled out than I think I ever have been before or since. Hearing footsteps wandering along the corridor outside, Jan popped his head in to see if we were finished and then showed me to my room, carrying a bottle of water, fresh towels and another plate of cheese.

I couldn't help but gasp in horror as he flicked the light on in what was to be my bedroom for the night.

'It's beautiful,' I smiled and tried to hide my shock at the scene before me. The most-relaxing-massage-of-all-time had already been undone, and I could feel my shoulders touching my earlobes in distress.

Dolls. Literally hundreds and hundreds of dolls. A floor-to-ceiling, wall-to-wall museum of creepy-looking dolls of all different sizes. Those with eyes were definitely following me around the room. However, it was the ones without the eyes I felt more concerned about. Apart from the bed itself, there wasn't a single flat surface that didn't have some uncanny collection of porcelain faces staring menacingly at me.

Jan seemed happy I was settled in and promptly left me alone with my new audience. I leapt into bed and clambered under the covers, feeling safe in the confidence of a small child who believed the monsters couldn't get me if I were tucked in tight. I could see the dolls clearly in the light of the almost full moon. *Great*, I thought, *I'm never going to sleep tonight.*

I woke naturally, feeling completely rested. Evidently, Maria's massage had not been entirely undone by horror-doll-central, and I took a long, full-body stretch before opening my eyes. I swear some of the dolls had moved.

Bidding Jan and Maria a fond farewell, I left feeling fully refreshed. It had been an interesting evening and one that I'll never forget. Jan and Maria were fantastic company, and the audience had (apart from my extra and unexpected new bandmate) been wonderfully supportive and encouraging. There'd even been a guy from the local press there who had smiled and stared at me all evening between scribbles. I felt great.

A week later, I received a copy of the article about my gig. In a scathing attack, the reporter stated that although I had apparently been 'reasonable to look at for a redhead,' he did not recommend attending any of my gigs.

Why? Because the harmonies (of my solo act) were 'uncomfortably atonal.'

Bridezilla and Dolly Parton

In walked a group of women in fancy dress: white thigh-high stiletto boots, mini-skirts, boob tubes, Sharpie-drawn eyebrows and huge back-combed hair. Except it wasn't fancy dress. It was Essex on a typical Friday night.

It was one of those Fridays when I wondered if I should be paying rent on the M25. Cars stuck in rush hour, crawling along at 2 miles per hour, encasing people leaving the desk jobs they hated, heading back to their houses they couldn't afford in a car they wouldn't need if they didn't have to get to the job they hated. But, much as I hated the M25, I was glad my time spent on it was limited compared to some poor pencil pushers. In my opinion, even the worst gigs in the world are marginally better than becoming a corporate drone.

We'd been asked if we could play some Country music in our set (because the regulars always asked for it) and had hastily learned *Jolene, Walk The Line* and *Friends In Low Places*. We figured we had a few bases covered there and hoped our attention to the landlord's request would guarantee us a rebooking. We even went to the effort of donning *double denim* and finding ourselves a couple of cowboy hats for the occasion.

It was late October and raining heavily when we arrived in Basildon. As we walked into the pub, we couldn't help but be utterly dumbstruck by the excess of gold tinsel adorning every single wall of the foyer. Christmas had come early in Essex, and the room glowed and sparkled with a nauseating yuletide gaud.

The locals seemed to enjoy our set: dancing, applauding and generally making us feel very welcome. The first set left us buzzing as we chatted with people at the bar during the break.

As we were just about to go back on, the smell of what I can only describe as *Tesco Value* perfume filled the room. It was cloying and overpowering. A pernicious stench that offended my eyes as well as my nose. I choked and turned to see where it was coming from.

Six young women walked in, looking like they had just come from a vicars and tarts party, leaving the vicars behind. The final girl to come into view was wearing a veil with an '*L plate.*' This was no fancy dress. This was an Essex girl hen night.

As they stumbled to the bar in outrageously high heels, it was hard to tell whether the girls were already drunk or had never walked in heels before. I stifled a giggle - mostly because I didn't want to breathe in as they got closer.

One of the girls threw herself at our guitarist, pulling at his hat as she lunged. He made a valiant attempt to catch her, but she was a big girl and landed on the floor with a bump rather than in his lap as intended. She stood up, ruffled, like a cat that had fallen off the windowsill and then looked around and tried to act as if she'd done it on purpose.

'You wanna watch 'er,' said the bride-to-be as she helped straighten her friend's boob tube. 'She'll steal yer 'at and sell it for drugs money.' Charming. As if that sentence wasn't bad enough, she followed it up with, 'like she did last week.'

Oh, Essex.

It was time for us to get back on stage, and somehow I managed to get enough air into my lungs to sing, despite the pungent cloud that hung in the air.

The second set was not received quite as well as the first. The locals had (understandably) mostly left by the time we went on. Having roughed up most of the men in the room, the hen group had effectively cleared the place. It was almost as if someone had played the bagpipes badly and told people they could only stay if they bought a ticket.

So, for our second set, we had just six wanna-be princesses as our audience.

'Play us some counnnnntreee music,' shouted one.

'Yeeeehaaaahhh,' yelled another.

Having already played all of our country songs in the first set, we realised everyone in the room, apart from the barmaid, was new since our first set, so we dutifully launched into *Jolene* for the second time that night.

'THAT'S NOT COUNTRY MUSIC, FOR FACK'S SAKE,' called the bride-to-be.
Being one of music history's most iconic country songs, I wasn't quite sure what to do next. Bridezilla was angry and abrasive; her bubblegum almost fell out of her mouth as she raged in disgust about Dolly Parton's lack of 'Countryness.'

'What kind of country music do you like, love?' I asked, trying not to stare as she picked at the ready-to-erupt blackhead on her chin.

'I like Meatloaf, innit. Play me some Meatloaf.'
I'm not sure Meatloaf would have considered himself a Country music artist, but the betrothed was adamant. I also wasn't sure that we were entirely set up to cover a full-blown rock opera artist like Meatloaf.

'It's my fackin' hen do, and you gotta do it cos aah said so.' She truly was a delight.

As I 'discussed' things with the bride-to-be, I noticed a young couple had sneaked in and sat at the back of the room. From how she was dressed, it was clear she wasn't part of the hen do. It would be fair to say that the striking difference between her and the other women in the room might lead you to believe that she was a librarian or a teacher from a Catholic school, perhaps. Outside of this pub, she probably looked completely normal, but here, she looked so out of place that she appeared prudish.

I couldn't help but notice that the couple were sitting, elbows on the table in front of them, smiling and watching the entire debacle unfold in front of them. We returned to our set when we finally quelled the conversation about Meatloaf from the all-out war on us down to some gentle muttering and sulking. Then, feeling the need for something to lift our spirits, we launched into one of our favourites from our *bad gigs list.*

'*Well, I don't know why I came here tonight,*' I sang as I winked at the couple at the back of the room, who were still absolutely entranced.
At the end of the evening, the couple came to speak to us as we were packing away. Introducing themselves as John and Julia, also engaged-to-be-married, John told us we were the perfect band for their forthcoming wedding, and if possible, they'd like to book us if we were available.

'That's very kind of you, but do you not think tonight was a bit of a disaster?' I asked, looking puzzled and frowning at them. Surely this wasn't what they wanted at their wedding.

Julia smiled the cheekiest of grins,

'I saw how you handled the audience tonight. I need someone with your balls to keep our families in check at our wedding.'

John and Julia's wedding was a whole lot of fun. Their families clearly hated each other but shared a bizarre love of Lindy hop dancing. Between bickering, they all came together for the faster songs from the set and joined arms, parading around the room as if they actually liked each other. It was magical.

Space hoppers and Zombies

'It'd be rude not to,' I grinned as I leapt onto one of the many space hoppers littering the green room that evening.

It had been a strange turn of events. After our evening with the Basildon hen party months earlier, we'd agreed it would be a shame to waste the handful of country songs we'd learned. So, in our true say-yes-then-figure-it-out-later fashion, we accepted a gig at a line dance club without the faintest idea of what to expect.

The club was held in the sports hall of a small village school in Middlesex. When we arrived, we were met by Jill, whom I assumed to be the lady in charge. Jill took us through to the hall, gestured at a huge raised stage, and through to the changing rooms at the back of the room.

'This is your room,' she waved as she opened the door to the boys changing rooms. It smelled of feet. Stale, teenage boy feet. About 30 pairs of them. But more importantly, there were space hoppers everywhere. Also, probably 30 of them. Big orange and blue space hoppers with smiling faces that all seemed to be looking at me and encouraging me to be a bit of a pickle as soon as Jill had gone.

'You can relax and change in here once you're set up. It's completely private, and no one will disturb you. You're on at 8.' With that, she half-curtseyed and turned tail. She was ever so formal, which seemed more than a little incongruous, given the overwhelming population of inflatable hippity hops.

I took a quick bounce around the changing room on a particularly friendly-looking space hopper and then decided we'd probably best get the stage set up and sound checked. Jill was busy putting out chairs around the room's edges and looked up, only to nod, half-smile, and continue busying herself organising everything.

As we were in the middle of sound check, Jill came over and asked us for our setlist. Scrutinising it carefully, she pulled out a pen tucked into her little grey ponytail and started tutting loudly.

'No,' she shouted, swiping her pen through the second song on the list.

'They won't like that.'

'No,' she said,

'That's too difficult to dance to.'

'No, definitely not that one, Glynnis will complain.'

It went on for what felt like an uncomfortable eternity. By the time she'd finished with our set list, it was covered in red pen scribbles where Jill had decided more than half of our songs were unsuitable for her club. I truly felt like I was back in school again.

'They will boo you if you try to play any of these,' said Jill, waving our defaced setlist at me.

I retreated to the green room to figure out what to do, knowing Jill had just scribbled out most of the entire list of country songs we knew, and knowing we definitely wouldn't have enough songs to fulfil our promise of two sets, we weren't sure what to do.

The rest of the band went to the stage to tidy cables, move cases off the stage and attempt to make the stage look appealing, even if all they were doing was setting us up for a boo-fest.

Taking the opportunity to change, I closed the changing room door and began removing my clothes. Jill flung open the door as I stood there in nothing but my underwear.

'No closed doors on the premises, please,' she yelled. I guessed she was one of the teachers from the way she could shout and her apparent lack of boundaries.

Knowing she'd already told me we would be undisturbed backstage, I stood, one hand on my hip and gestured,

'So, these are my tits!' I said calmly, not breaking my stare.

Jill's face turned scarlet.

'Cover yourself, woman,' she said as I stood there defiantly.

'What on earth is wrong with you?' yelled Jill, now attempting to throw a feet-scented towel at me to cover mysel

'I was assured that my dressing room was private.' I gestured again and wiggled a little, surprising myself at my unusual absence of self-loathing.

Rather than back down, Jill described me as an 'unacceptable whore.' The mistake had apparently been mine for not realising Jill excluded herself from the privacy rule she had created purely because, as I found out later, she was the headmistress.

'Come in and close the door behind you,' I spoke quietly, despite my frustration. Throwing on a t-shirt, I smiled and gestured for her to sit beside me. Now was my chance to fix the evening.

Jill rolled her eyes at me, possibly assuming I, the whore I am, was about to jump her.

'I think it best if we play the songs on our set list without removing the ones you've scribbled out.' I didn't break my stare.

'Do we have a deal?'

'They won't like it,' she huffed as she stood, tripped over a stray space hopper and launched herself headfirst out the door.

The main hall slowly filled with people: almost exclusively women dressed in rhinestone-covered outfits, *Poundland*'s finest cowboy hats and plasticky-looking cowboy boots. Each person arrived and then sat around the edge of the room, leaving the dance floor completely empty. It looked a little sad.

We burst onto the stage and tried to raise the energy in the room. Everyone sat totally still. After a couple of bars of the first song, people started to get up from their seats and shuffled onto the dance floor - each dancer copying a leader at the front.

It looked a little like the music video accompanying Michael Jackson's, Thriller. Zombie-looking women shuffled around, clapped, did *jazz hands* for a second, spun around, clapped again, and kicked their heels together. Not one of them raised a smile. On the contrary, they all looked thoroughly miserable.

At the end of the first song, the room erupted in applause. It felt good.

And then they all sat back down again. Oh!

This happened after every single song for the entire evening. I learned later that line dancers like to get a feel for the beat before they get up to dance, hence the two or three bars of shuffle-less activity at the start of each song. Nonetheless, they applauded warmly after every song, even the ones Jill said they wouldn't like. Even the one Glynnis would complain about (whomever the hell Glynnis was).

Jill never spoke to us again. At the end of the evening, a swarm of the night's zombies stood around us, asking when we'd be coming back again, all saying that it was the best evening they'd had at the club in years. Amid all the positivity from the club members, Jill thrust our fee for the night into my hand and left.

We didn't get to play there again. While packing up the van, I overheard Jill telling a group of women that I had been 'disrespectful and obscene' and that she wouldn't be booking us again.

Beans and pizza

The instructions were very detailed. *DO NOT FOLLOW YOUR GPS; you will get lost. Instead, turn left where Beans Cafe used to be.* Except, I'd never visited this part of Germany before and the idea of giving directions to turn left where something used to be struck me as a little unhelpful.

The gig, a house concert, had been in the diary for about a year, and I'd received regular updates from Geert, the host, from the moment we'd agreed on the date. He wrote to tell me about the weather, the roads, the wildlife in his garden and lots more exciting stories about his and his wife's off-grid life. It was fascinating. The only problem was that my only previous experience of the name 'Geert' had been during my GCSE German lessons, where, for whatever reason, our teacher had decided we needed to be able to say the phrase 'Geert needs a raincoat.' If I recall correctly, there was a whole Janet and John-type book about poor Geert's plight. So every time I received an email from Geert, I couldn't help but think of him in a gigantic yellow Mackintosh.

Geert (the real one, not the German GCSE one) lived in a very rural cabin-in-the-woods-style property in Northern Germany. He was what you might call a Proper Woodsman. By all accounts, Geert spent his days chopping wood and preparing for the winters while his wife, Liesl, found novel and exciting ways to preserve their abundant fruit and vegetable harvests.

I'd been very much looking forward to meeting Geert and Liesl, and their emails had become increasingly frequent the closer it got to the gig date. Lots of last-minute details I probably didn't need but still stashed away in my tour folder just in case. Included within my (now heaving) folder was a double-sided printout of directions from the main highway to their rural property. At the top of the page, in bright red large print, it said, 'DO NOT FOLLOW YOUR GPS.' The directions, in small print, went on forever, and I had to keep stopping to double-check them.

'Turn right at the tumbledown barn'. I don't know if you've ever driven through Germany, but tumbledown barns are quite a feature of the countryside and really not something to give important directions by. It'd be a little like providing directions in England as 'turn right at the oak tree' or 'keep left at the empty McDonalds wrapper'. Not helpful.

I reached a village that was no more than a crossroads with a small post office, and I pulled over to read the next instruction: 'Turn left where Beans Cafe used to be.' *'Oh great!'* I thought, *'That's even less helpful.'*

I got out of the car and wandered around the village, looking for any sign of Beans or cafes anywhere. No luck. Stepping up the rickety wooden staircase, I pushed hard on the heavy wooden door to the *Deutsche Post* and hoped someone there spoke English.

A teenage girl stood behind the counter, her pink hair spiked and gelled to within an inch of its life. Her make-up was heavy and almost clown-like, and I wondered if I'd temporarily stepped into 1981.

'Sprechen sie English?' I ventured, with my very minimal *'get by'* German. I'd never enjoyed German at school. Thanks to my GCSE German teacher, I spoke German with a strong Scottish accent, so I tended to shy away from attempting to converse in German unless I absolutely had to. This was definitely one of those 'have-to' occasions.

'I do,' said the girl. I gestured my relief with an overdramatic wipe of the forehead and asked her if she knew where Beans Cafe used to be.

'Oh, Beans closed before I was born, but there is a cafe miles this way,' she pointed her two fingers up and then gestured in the direction of the cafe I wasn't looking for.

'No, I mean, do you know where Beans *used* to be?' I tried again, emphasising *'used'* to get my point across.

The girl looked confused and began pulling at one of the spikes in her hair, making it droop slightly.

'No, Beans is not there. It. Closed. Down,' she repeated looking at me as if she thought perhaps my English wasn't very good.

Smiling back at her, I tried again to explain that I had been given directions which involved turning left where Beans used to be. The girl grew visibly agitated, and I decided to leave, nodding and repeating, 'My mistake, my mistake,' as I closed the door firmly behind me.

I was likely running late if I didn't find the Beans Cafe burial site soon. There was only one thing for it. I plugged my GPS in and put Geert's address into it. At worst, it should get me closer to his house, and perhaps I could find someone else to pester, or maybe I might finally pick up a phone signal and be able to call and admit defeat.

My GPS took me precisely to Geert's house. The whiny-voiced Irish woman said, 'You have arrived at your destination,' just as I spotted the picturesque little cottage in the woods that I'd been sent so many photos of over the past year.

Geert must have seen me pull into the driveway and came rushing out, his long grey hair flowing behind him, with Liesl tailing not far behind. They looked the picture of rural living with clothes intended for comfort, not style, wearing huge black Wellington boots and seeming totally at one with their beautiful surroundings.

Geert stretched out his long wiry arms and crouched a little to hug me. He was outrageously tall. A huge smile crept across his face as he congratulated himself for giving me such precise instructions.

'Our house is so hard to find, and I just don't trust that these new-fangled GPS devices have the capacity to know where I live out here in the middle of nowhere. Besides,' he said, looking anxiously over his shoulder, 'I don't want Them to know where I live.'

'Right-ho,' I said as I breezed over what looked like a hot topic was about to be discussed. I didn't mention to him how precise the GPS had been, nor how daft his directions were. He seemed like a nice chap, and besides, he was busy firing up a gigantic outdoor pizza oven, and who was I to argue with a man making pizza?

Liesl showed me to the bathroom and my bedroom for the night and then took me on the Grand Tour. Being my first experience of a genuinely off-grid home, Liesl took great delight and pride in showing me all the features: the solar panels on the roof, the vegetable garden, her canning station, her stash of echinacea and various other medicinal plants and most intriguingly, the indoor compost toilet. I tried not to look too much into it, really I did, but there were absolutely no unpleasant odours emanating from it at all, and it looked from my minimal inspection that it went as deep as the centre of the earth. This was no Glastonbury toilet. This was a classy loo which, if it hadn't been for the lack of flush handle and extreme draft on your bits as you sit down, you'd never have known.

I set up to play in a large, open-plan greenhouse-like room. Long, low benches for the audience to sit on were laid out in rows. Spider plants had taken over every wall and dangled precariously from little hooks in the ceiling. As I milled about, drifting towards the smells emanating from the pizza oven, more and more elderly hippy-types arrived, each greeting me with a warm patchouli-scented hug.

The gig was great and mostly uneventful. I did explode into some kind of involuntary coughing fit at one point during the first set and had to stop playing while I gestured the international hand signal for '*I'm going to die, please bring water.*' A large bald man brought a glass towards me but tripped on a loose tie-dyed rug as he neared the front and successfully gave me a quick shower rather than the sip of water I'd so clearly gestured for. As he landed, glass held high to try to rescue some of the water, I noticed he wasn't bald at all. Instead, a very long wispy grey plait came directly out of the middle of the back of his head and reached almost to his waist. We all gave a round of applause when it was clear he wasn't hurt, and he stood up, bowed, handed me the mostly empty glass, and sat back quietly in his seat.

The whole afternoon was genuinely heartwarming. Geert, Liesl and their friends were exhilarating company. Almost all of them spoke excellent English, and those who didn't damn well tried almost as much as I tried to speak German to them. We shared pizza and wine, and I thoroughly enjoyed everyone's company.

The festivities continued long after I packed away and well into the night. Despite being in an off-grid home in the middle of a foreign country, I felt completely relaxed and welcome.

As I was making my apologies to the stragglers who had stayed longer than my eyelids had made plans for, I overheard one couple chatting.

Did you hear that Beans Cafe closed down?'

As I stepped slowly backwards, heading towards my room, I realised that in a community this rural, who only get together to drink copious amounts of homemade wine, it may be the only news item that has happened in the area in (I'm guessing from the age of the girl in the post office) about 15 years.

Hot Chocolate and Rock Stars

'I did everything short of running naked up and down the street, shouting about your gig. We just can't get people to come out.'

I winced as I knew exactly what line was coming next,

'It's a funny town.'

Ah, there it is. Word for word.

I've heard it before and hope never to hear it again. But I've heard it so often that I genuinely believe there is a *Bad Promoter Phrase Book* on the black market. Pauline ran a tiny failing venue in a town of about 5,000 people in the South of Scotland, only an hour from Edinburgh. Pauline's place had 30 seats and was what I would call a *filler gig* en route to another venue. It was the kind of place whose name didn't match its size: Something like the South Scotland Stadium or The Northern Arena. Very grandiose considering it was a shoebox. But it had a beautiful little self-contained apartment upstairs which Pauline kindly let the bands use. Together with a home-cooked meal and everything needed for me to throw together a decent-sized full English-border breakfast, it seemed like a good spot for a filler gig. It was perfectly placed to be en route to almost anywhere in Scotland.

The tour was during peak season, so rather than book a pricey hotel, it made sense to play for Pauline, regardless of the lack of an audience. Pauline was yet another venue owner at breaking point. She'd obviously bought the place on a whim, perhaps a mid-life crisis, and spent more time painting it in funky colours, giving it a grandiose name and making it look cool than actually making inroads into the community in any attempt to let people know that the quaint little town-house that occasionally has a small poster in the window is actually a 30 seat music venue.

Pauline's venue was never full. She used the usual BINGO phrases, *'it depends on the band'* and *'it's a funny town,'* but week in, week out, her personal social media complained about the town's lack of community spirit. The venue page never posted any updates and had laid dormant for over three years.

The street outside the venue was between two trendy touristy restaurants. As I stood listening to Pauline telling me she was thinking of calling it a day and buying a B&B instead, I wondered if I could salvage the evening. I have a big pop-up banner for just this kind of occasion, and despite being on the North Sea coast, it was a surprisingly breeze-free day - perfect for putting the banner up and maybe attracting a few last-minute audience members. There was really nothing to lose.

As all 5 feet of me stood wrestling with the 6-foot banner, a couple walked past and stopped to watch as I struggled.

'Is this you?' asked the lady as I stood next to a full-size version of me.

'Are you performing here?'

'Yup,' I replied with a big smile.

'Tonight?' asked the man, as he stared straight at the banner which said, 'Performing here tonight' in big, bold red letters above my head.

'Yup,' I grinned again.

'Oh, that's a shame,' said the woman, 'we can't make it tonight. Can you do it tomorrow instead?'

I wondered silently what went through someone's mind when they asked questions like these. I didn't have an answer. I was on tour, travelling from venue to venue. I was on a deadline that didn't really involve telling everyone already inside the venue that we'd have to reschedule the gig for tomorrow.

For some inexplicable reason, advertising a) that the venue existed and b) that there was music in it tonight gave Pauline her first ever 'sold out' show in her three years of business. She put it down to me having lots of fans and being well-known in the area. She re-booked me on the spot.

The gig itself was fine. Pauline did indeed have a lovely little community in her little tourist town. As my accommodation was upstairs, I was all packed up and ready to call it a night by 10 p.m., so I pottered off for some downtime before a long drive the next day.

Curled up under a substantial fluffy velvet blanket on a gigantic sofa, sipping some hot chocolate, I flicked on the TV and began watching The Doors movie. Watching the levels of drug taking, hookers, late nights and booze, I wondered if perhaps I was getting touring wrong.

Peanut butter sandwiches and difficult women

Standing in a room full of double beds strewn with tie-dye-clad bodies amidst a cloud of pungent smoke, I very quickly realised there had, perhaps, been a slight misunderstanding about the plan for this evening.

The stench enveloped the room so much that I began to crave biscuits. The second-hand smoke was overwhelming, and I began to feel lightheaded and sick.

'That's your bed,' said Eric the promoter, pointing to a small double bed with a single pillow and a couple of raggedy-looking blankets. The three of us didn't know whether to laugh or cry. This was our first introduction to Netherlands hospitality, and so far, it wasn't quite meeting expectations.

We'd discussed the gig with Eric via email in great detail during the past few months. From his descriptions, it sounded like it would be a dream gig. One where the audience pays a ticket price and sits and listens with (his words) 'pin-drop attentiveness.' He was to provide food and accommodation for the night, all of the door money would go to the band, and the venue had a capacity of about 150. It sounded right up our street. We should have known better.

We'd discussed set lists, our requirements for accommodation (3 single girls), and the severe food allergy to nuts that one of the band had. We felt heard and respected and were excited about the prospect of an attentive audience and a very accommodating host.

I plonked myself down on *our* bed while Eric scurried off to be a gracious host to the people who were arriving early. As I sat, I felt one of the springs dig mercilessly into my thigh. Pulling back the covers, I noticed several coils of wire poking through the thin sheets. I didn't want to appear ungrateful, but I was starting to wonder if Eric wasn't entirely as bilingual as he'd implied in his messages.

We trudged downstairs and began setting up in the corner of the room. I always try to mingle and meet a few audience members before gigs. I find it helps me connect more deeply with audiences and nourishes my soul. I've always done it and I always will. I thoroughly relish the opportunity. Usually.

Once we were set up, I wandered into the group of people milling around the plates of sandwiches and began trying to introduce myself. For every new person I smiled at, there was Eric, swooping in like a vulture, asking me what I wanted. Each time, I transferred my attention from the audience member to Eric, politely letting him know I was just making new friends and didn't need anything. This seemed to irk Eric no end. His behaviour towards me was like that of a wayward work experience kid who was bothering the customers. Finally, after about ten repetitions of this little dance, I gave up and asked him if we could perhaps help ourselves to some of the food.

Eric didn't speak. He rolled his eyes and gestured towards the table. I was too hungry to be bothered to say anything but 'thank you' and excitedly headed for the table, planning to fill my pie-hole before we were due to start playing.

When I reached the table, each plate of sandwiches had a little cocktail stick flag to tell you what filling you were to expect. My knowledge of the Dutch language extends to the following phrases;

'One beer, please' and 'Another beer, please.'

Each sandwich had the word *pindakaas* in it, so I assumed this was the Dutch for 'sandwich.' Other than that, all I could ascertain was that these were not beer sandwiches.

Deciding to ignore Eric's vulture-like swooping, I spoke to a group of what looked like young backpackers to see if any of them spoke English. A thin blonde girl whose hairstyle resembled someone who had been camping for most of her life nodded at me, smiling widely and displaying the contents of her sandwich.

Luckily, Anje's English was perfect, and I didn't have to figure out the sandwich fillings from the half-eaten mush coating her front teeth. She kindly talked me through every plate on the table;

'This one is peanut butter and tomato, this is peanut butter and jam, this one over here is peanut butter and cucumber, and here we have some peanut butter and chocolate spread.'

Eric, the vulture, was making a beeline for me, presumably to let me know I was bothering the guests again, but this time I was prepared for him.

'What do you want with the guests?' he asked in such a stern way that I couldn't tell was annoyance or just his general manner. I asked him if there were any sandwiches that didn't have *pindakaas* in them. I felt almost fluent now that I knew an extra word - especially a life-threatening one.

Eric threw up his arms in the air in melodramatic annoyance. To this day, I don't know whether he thought our previous discussions about 'serious peanut allergy' were misconstrued as an obsessive love of peanuts or whether he had been deliberately obstreperous. Either way, he announced loudly to his backpacking friends that nothing was good enough for the 'difficult English girls' and told us we should get on with the music. In a show of solidarity and out of concern for singing with peanut breath at each other, we all went on hungry.

It quickly became apparent that Eric's idea of a pin-drop audience differed slightly from ours. At one point, a food fight ensued amongst the young and increasingly rowdy 'listeners,' which escalated into them chanting at each other louder and louder until one stood up and everyone cheered. Something about their behaviour and the general demeanour made me think it was not very likely they'd paid any ticket price. I began to get concerned that we were about to get into an argument and be seen as even more 'difficult.'

In the break, I sought out Eric and broached the subject of payment with him. He pointed to a hat on the *pindakaas* table of death and said that if we were 'good enough,' people could put money in the hat. Oh, how I detest 'hat gigs.'

Taking matters into my own hands, I walked around with the hat in my hand, asking people to contribute. Unfortunately, if the events in the dormitory upstairs were anything to go by, most people in the room were too stoned to have any idea that music was happening, let alone that we had been promised payment.

My suspicions were correct. One dreadlocked girl looked at me and asked,

'Do I look like I have money?' Honestly? No, she didn't. Not two euros to rub together. She said that if I wanted to, I could have her 'crusty knickers' as payment.

I marvelled at her command of the English language and her ability to induce instant nausea in another person by using her second language as a biological weapon. Then, raising up a silent prayer of thanks that I had no food in my belly to expel, I politely but firmly declined.

Later in the break, a young, bearded man came up to me and asked me my most favourite dumb question of ALL TIME:

'Are you sure that's a saxophone?' Am I sure? Am I sure about the instrument I play professionally? The glassy red-eyed look told me that there was no point entering into a debate so I summoned up my favourite off-the-cuff response of ALL TIME:

'Well, I bought it on eBay and you never can tell with eBay. Perhaps it isn't.' Simple. Easy. Job done. No one was made to feel foolish. I wandered off, grinning to myself, thinking what a great title that would be for a book.

Going back on for the second set was one of the most demoralising moments on stage in my entire career. By the end of the break, the hat looked like it had about 20 euros in it. Less than it would cost us in petrol to get to the next gig, and considering this had looked as though it was going to be the highlight of the tour, my frame of mind was in no mood for any more shit from Eric and his crusty-knickered-backpackers.

About 20 minutes into the second set, amidst the screams, I pulled off a solo that must have impressed one of my bandmates enough that she called out my name, encouraging the audience to cheer.

Crickets.

No one responded. No one looked up. No one so much as raised a smile. We'd all had enough and were starving and demoralised. I stopped playing, and right there on stage midway through my solo, calmly into the microphone, I whispered,

'Nope. I'm done.'
My fabulous bandmates agreed, and we called it a day. No one noticed. We packed up our gear. No one noticed. We carried our gear through the crowd to the door, bashing kneecaps and ankles as we went. No one noticed. We took the full 22 Euros (plus three buttons, two gum wrappers and a paperclip) from the hat. No one noticed. We drove off into the night in search of a pindakaas-free drive-thru and a motel. No one noticed.

This was more than fifteen years ago. I often wonder if they've noticed yet.

A funny-shaped pub and a tip I didn't earn

When you're called to play a gig at a pub that the locals lovingly call, *The Small Cock* you know it's probably a good idea to get paid the moment you walk in the door rather than at the end of the gig when the landlord is too drunk or drugged up to remember that you were even there.

We'd been warned about *The Small Cock* by fellow musicians. We talk, you know. A couple of people had written to me out of the blue when I announced the gig on social media to warn us that the landlord was a 'shady character' and that drug raids and juicy gossip were the order of the day. Not to mention that some of the road names nearby were things like *Stabbed Woman Lane* and *Ladyshot Avenue*. I wasn't sure about this area of Essex at the best of times, but it was en route between a couple of decent gigs, so we threw it in the diary and wondered what's the worst that could happen.

When we arrived, the only person in the pub was the barmaid. I would describe her attire as Middle-Ages-wench-chic and wondered whether it was a uniform or her own personal sense of style. She greeted us warmly, paid us in cash and told us to set up in what she called *the Middle Bar*. She then asked if we'd be OK with 'minding the place' until the landlord came downstairs from his nap. Before we got the chance to reply, she'd already left.

The pub had a strange layout: long and thin with three distinct areas. The entrance hall at the front with a large sunny patio and smoking area, the central area where we set up, and a room at the back of the pub with a large TV and a pool table. We were due to play to the Sunday Lunch crowd, so I wondered why we'd been set up in the middle room, which we saw as a kind of purgatory between the patio and the TV.

As we set up, Kevin, the landlord, emerged from upstairs. Yawning loudly and stretching his arms out over-dramatically, Kevin walked straight past us and put the football on loudly in the next room. Then, returning only to pour himself a pint at the bar and grab a few packets of crisps he plonked himself down in front of the TV without even so much as a nod in our direction.

We were due to start playing at 1 pm and at about 5 minutes to, we were thrilled to see a large group of people arriving at the pub. Initially, of course, we assumed they were there for the live music, but as each of them walked past us with the same disdain the landlord had shown, we slowly realised they were all here for something unrelated to us: the football on the big screen.

Feeling slightly demoralised, the two of us were standing chatting about the setlist when the landlord got up from his sofa, poured another beer, and gestured over at us,

'You can start if you like.'

I guess we start then.

The side of the bar with the football was heaving. Pints were raised, cheers were loudly directed at the TV, and everyone looked to be having a great time. If I stepped off the stage area, I could see the bar, but I couldn't if I stepped back on it. Which meant they also couldn't see me. I was pretty confident they couldn't hear me either.

The bar wrapped all the way along the pub, so there was no need for anyone in the TV room to come through our area for more beers. The only time anyone walked through was on their way to the smoking area on the patio outside.

We launched into a Stealers Wheel number and grinned at each other while I sang,

'Well, I don't know why I came here tonight.'

I stopped. I really didn't know why we *came here tonight*. We both giggled loudly and realised we could probably get away with absolutely anything. No one was paying any attention to us at all. Not to mention, we'd already been paid.

I'm not proud of what happened next. I usually take my job very seriously, even if no one else around me does, but on this one occasion, we deemed it necessary to conduct an experiment.

So between us, we concocted an evil plan to see just how little time we could get away with actually playing. It was easy to see if someone was about to walk through, and we could happily throw together a rousing line or two from the setlist when needed. We even decided to make the game more fun by not discussing what song we would *perform* next, leaving me to guess from the chord sequence or make something up on the spot. For two hours, we played in ten-second bursts. Again, I'm not proud of this. Well, maybe a little. No one noticed.

Eventually, we sang one more '*Well, I don't know why I came here tonight*' and called it a day.

As we began packing the gear, Kevin must have seen us moving around and popped out to thank us for such a great show. Shaking us both warmly by the hand, he told us that everyone who'd come through from the beer garden had been commenting on how enjoyable our music was. He even offered us a £50 tip (which my then hugely guilty conscience refused) and asked if we'd be happy to return in a couple of months because we'd been 'such a hit with the locals.'

We hadn't played a single complete song.

Football and fisticuffs

The evening had started reasonably well. Mike, the owner, welcomed us warmly and told us that once we were set up, we could order whatever we wanted from the menu—his treat. Our drummer was positively drooling at the 5-gallon jar of Tabasco sauce he spotted through the kitchen door.

It was a typical Saturday night in South London. The pub was loud, and the TV was playing footage of a football match at full blast. Beers were raised, glasses were chinked together, and everyone seemed in high spirits. My mood for the evening was helped very much by several waitresses dancing on the tables during our soundcheck: even when we were just sound-checking the kick drum. It seemed as though the evening was shaping up to be a good one.

We were set up at the far end of the pub. There was a large dance floor in front of us, and the bar ran all down the left-hand side of the long, galley-like space. To the right was a separate area for diners. Once we'd finished entertaining the waitresses with our soundcheck, we wandered to the dining area and thoroughly enjoyed an outstanding amount of genuine pub grub.

The pub was shoulder to shoulder with (I'm no good with numbers, but) a million people, all of whom were significantly taller than me and saw no reason to move out of the way to let me through. As a result, the arduous journey from the restaurant to the stage took what felt like forever, and I arrived on stage with both bruised elbows and a bruised ego.

We stood on stage for about ten minutes, signalling Mike to turn off the volume on the big screen TVs that boomed around the room and elicited deafening jeers and cheers depending on whose side each punter was on. The volume didn't change, and eventually, Mike came over to ask why we hadn't started playing.

'We can't hear ourselves, so I'm guessing they won't hear us either,' yelled our drummer. 'Can you turn the volume off on the TVs?'
Mike looked at us as if we'd gone completely mad.

'I'll get lynched,' he said incredulously. 'It's the Millwall match... you'll have to make do.'

So, turning our speakers up as loudly as we could on stage so that we could at least hear each other, we launched into our first song. I'm not even sure if we were all playing the same song - it was so loud that all I could hear was yelling from the audience and the occasional snare drum from behind me.

We decided it would be one of those gigs that, well, I write about years later, and we just got our heads down and got on with it. We were being paid to play music. The fact that no one could hear said music was irrelevant.

As we were playing what turned out to be the last song of the night, I had a brief moment where I'd managed to shut out the fact that we were in a rough South London pub surrounded by far too many extremely drunk and increasingly aggressive football fans. I'd forgotten that I was at least a foot shorter than everyone else in the bar, and I was just relaxing and getting into the music. Singing my head off with my eyes shut, I became suddenly aware that the band had stopped dead in the middle of the song.

Opening my eyes, all I could see were fists. I looked behind me to see the drummer with a huge hooded guy sitting in his lap and another equally menacing-looking dude hurtling uncontrollably towards our guitarist.

Looking up at our 40kg speakers swaying unpredictably above me, I leapt over to the mixer desk and turned it to full volume. Running back to the front of the stage area, shoving the odd Millwall fan out of the way, I grabbed my wireless mic and pointed it at the monitor. Cue HOWLING feedback.

I'd finally got Mike's attention, and he decided now was the time to turn off the TVs. Unfortunately, everyone else in the pub decided this was their signal to launch into a collective Millwall-fan-tantrum of epic proportions. Things were getting serious. I didn't feel safe.

Our drummer was sat on his (now broken) stool, fending people off with a shattered drumstick. The guitars and my saxes were safely away in their cases (but not without having suffered some dents and scratches), the kick drum skin was ripped in half, and the snare drum had someone sitting in it, so I figured that was probably done for too.

Climbing onto the bass bin, I held my wireless mic up to the front of house speaker. It let out an almighty whoop of feedback, even louder than the previous, causing pretty much everyone in the room to rush to cover their ears. The fighting stopped, and everyone looked in our direction silently. Putting the mic up to my mouth and quietly saying 'thank you' was all that was needed to make the Millwall supporters cower like little naughty schoolboys in the Headmaster's office.

The guy who had first landed in the drummer's lap had disappeared out the pub's back door. It was his arrival that had sparked the fight - some kind of Millwall mentality rivalry or something. Either way, he was long gone, so most of the troublemakers decided they might as well go looking for him in the next pub, street, or wherever - I didn't care so long as they left us out of it.

The pub cleared quickly after that, and Mike came over and apologised, handed me some cash, and said he'd love to book us again - perhaps in three months or so. He helped us load all of our gear into the van, and just as we'd finished packing everything up, our drummer told Mike we'd be in touch once we'd had the equipment damage assessed in more detail.

Mike looked blank,

'Damage?' he asked as if it was the first he was hearing of it.

'Yes,' he replied, looking a little confused, 'the drum kit took a nasty hit, and a couple of guitars have some dents and scratches.' Mike continued to look confused,

'How did that happen?'

I was bewildered and wondered if Mike was a little worse for wear himself.

'Because of the fight,' I replied.

'No one fights in my pub,' said Mike, his arms folded.

'You're making stuff up to try and get more money out of me.' He waved his fist at me and said that he'd given us 'plenty of cash' as well as a 'free meal' and that we were 'ungrateful shits'. Then, he stormed back inside and locked the door behind himself.

The following morning, Fulham made the National news when it was reported that a man had met with a *freak accident*. Citing the injury as 'bewildering' and 'life-threatening,' the man had somehow managed to impale both legs on iron railings 8ft off the ground whilst 'out for a jog.'

Welcome to South London.

And there's more...

More often than not, a gig will go fine, but there will be just one thing that isn't worthy of an entire story but is still very much worthy of mention. So here are a few...ready?

'I could have been a musician, but the drink and drugs would have killed me.' A host after a gig in Newcastle. No amount of telling her that they're not obligatory would change her mind.

'There is a shortage of Blu-Tack in this town.' This was an actual answer to my question about why the promoter hadn't put up our posters.

'No, don't stop; you're barely annoying anyone.' A barman at the half-time point of a gig in Sussex.

'I thought you said you'd hired a publicist.' An irate venue owner after we'd hired a publicist who didn't understand her job title.

'I could have been a musician, but I have a very high-powered proper job.' A guy in a bar in Berkshire

The couple at the bar are discussing what music we are listening to in the break. She says it's Oasis, and he says it is heavy metal. It is Jack Johnson.

I was setting up for a gig once, and a 6-year-old boy was in front of the stage holding his crotch and gyrating Michael Jackson style. When his father finally arrived, he joined in.

I sat at the bar once, listening to two men arguing whether today was the 30th or the 31st of December. They both agreed it was New Year's Eve, though.

The night an audience member told me I was pretty good and asked if I knew ALL the notes. When I told him I knew both G sharp AND A flat, he looked impressed and bought an album.

The time a venue asked me what a duo was. I responded, 'It's a two-piece band,' to which he replied... 'Oh... a band....and how many people are there in the band?'

Band wanted for our wedding (at least six piece). We want the extra special touch. We want you to be able to play anything we request. We want a band of full-time professional musicians of an excellent standard to play for a minimum of 6 hours. Payment details will be decided on the day but will probably cover travel expenses—a genuine advert in my local newspaper.

'Will the bump show in the wedding photos?'
'I hope not. It's the best man's.' Overheard in the ladies at a wedding.

Internet trolls and semitones

There is always one. Without fail, there is always at least one. Whatever you do or say on the internet, you will find that one troll who has nothing in their life but to argue with strangers and deliberately make people feel bad with their own self-absorbed nonsense.

A few years back, and more recently than all of the other stories in this book, I shared a performance video on Facebook. It created a very-very-very-mini-viral storm for a couple of weeks. The video was of our version of a well-known song. I was pretty pleased with the solos I'd pulled off and was revelling in the shower of positivity that I was receiving. As an artist, short of cold hard cash, very little makes us drop the self-doubts more quickly than fan and peer recognition.

The video was being shared worldwide, and the comments were pouring in. I was truly buzzing. 'This is the best cover ever,' and 'That is some stunning sax playing.' Comments were racking up on the video, and within a week, it had been viewed almost a quarter of a million times and with thousands of positive comments. I was truly on a life-affirming high. Total strangers had taken time out of their busy lives to like, share and make all sorts of delightful comments that made my soul soar.

Until Karl. I don't know who Karl is. A middle-aged man with a porn star moustache who was holding an electric guitar in his profile picture and smiling smugly at the camera. Karl was up for taking me down a few pegs.

'I cannot understand the appeal of this god-awful noise. The solo is a semi-tone sharp all the way through (and I should know, I'm a saxophone player). This video has ruined music for all time for me.'

I looked at the comment amidst the sea of positive comments, and the self-doubt crept predictably in. What is it about being a creative person that means that you can get a thousand positive responses to your work, but the one that isn't positive is the one that you focus obsessively on? Why would Karl go to such lengths to hurt a total stranger? Maybe it *was* as bad as he said. My mind spiralled until I got a hold of myself and remembered ...*Troll Mentality.*

I was sorely tempted to re-record my solo a semitone flat and re-post it for my own amusement. I can't imagine a single musician in the world, whatever their level, who could knowingly play an entire solo a whole semi-tone out without them recognising it sounds truly awful. It made me think of the comedy genius of Tim Mincin's F Sharp song. It simply isn't possible.

'*DON'T FEED THE TROLLS,*' I reminded myself. I'd seen this kind of thing plenty of times before and decided to just click like on his comment. I knew that would likely rile him, but I didn't give him anything to get his teeth into to continue his diatribe. I wanted him to know I'd seen his comment and wanted him to believe he hadn't affected me.

After clicking *like*, my constant-searching-for-approval brain then clicked on Karl's profile, which was completely public.

His most recent status gave me an insight,

'Excited that I've been learning the F chord today. Won' have to sit that one out at Open Mic before too long.'

I read on... 'My manager has got me a gig!! Yess!! Busking in Tooting Broadway Underground Station on Saturday.'

Further down the page, Karl shared a video of himself singing a Bob Dylan song and playing the guitar (out of tune and out of time) along with it. It took everything I had not to comment that he had 'ruined music for all time for me.' I'm all for supporting other musicians, and I relish constructive criticism, but not from dicks.

Dead fish and roadkill

Sometimes you get to be the K*night in Shining Armour.* Sometimes you get to be the *Damsel in Distress.* One evening, I ended up being both, falling from the lofty heights title of *the-person-who-saved-the-day* to what had felt briefly like *front-page-of-the-Eastbourne-Gazette-murder-victim.*

Late one Friday night, I received a call from a very distraught bride-to-be. She explained, through various wailing noises, sniffling, swearing and sobbing, that the band she had booked for her wedding tomorrow had pulled out. She'd stumbled across my name in the local Yellow Pages as, at the time, one of my gigs was a solo act where I performed at weddings, birthday parties, retirement homes and the like, and it was an excellent place to advertise.

Kirsty, the bride, wanted some live music at her wedding. She didn't care what, she didn't care who or how many were in the band or what style of music it was, she just wanted something (anything) for her special day.

I did my best to reassure her that I could happily perform my solo set for her. But unfortunately, despite having called a solo performer, this didn't reassure her at all. She wanted a full band to play for at least four hours with less than 24 hours notice, and I was doing my best, but I could feel Bride-Zilla might be about to emerge.

'OK,' I said, 'I have an idea,' doing my best to pacify the imminent eruption. I was working with a Madness tribute band at the time. I knew we had nothing in the diary for the next day. Another band member also had a solo act, so I suggested that between the two solo sets and the tribute band, we could put together four hours of live music. The two solo sets would be performed during the meals and between speeches, and the band would be there for dancing later in the evening.

Bride-Zilla's wailing was reduced to some light whimpering, and she cautiously agreed that this could work.

We swapped details, agreed on a fee, and I went to call around the band to double-check that everyone was OK with the idea. All in. Great! I called Kirsty back to confirm.

Kirsty's wedding was a kind of Essex affair attempting to look fancy. It all felt a little bit like going to Poundstretcher for the weekly shop and carrying it all home in Waitrose bags. It was a nice enough hotel on the seafront overlooking a typical English seaside town scene with arcades, blue and white striped deck chairs and menacing seagulls poised to swoop in and steal your chips. Kirsty, however, was your typical Essex girl. With a powerful cockney-like belt, she could be heard from anywhere in the hotel.

Someone had had the bright idea that having a live goldfish in a bowl on each table would be nice. A fancy-looking centrepiece that all of Kirsty's friends and family could marvel at and 'ooh' and 'aah' over how posh everything looked. Unfortunately, no one had told whoever set up the unique centrepieces that you can't just drop a goldfish into a bowl of tap water and expect the selfish creature not just to go ahead and die. So there, in this beautifully decorated hotel room, was a series of miniature aquatic graveyards with floating fish corpses.

'What the FAAAAAAACK is wrong with the FAAAACKIN' fish?' said our dainty little bride. Kirsty plunged her hand into one of the bowls, pulled out a dead fish and held it above her head.

'Everything's ruined,' she sank to her knees with the fish still held tightly between her hands.

The groom chose this moment to make an entrance—a quiet and unassuming man with a nondescript look. Despite searching him up and down for what felt like probably too long, I couldn't find anything to distinguish him from a cardboard cut-out of a not-very-interesting man. Nonetheless the groom (I never did catch his name) did a great job of placating Bride-Zilla, and the pair of them wandered to the bar, arm in arm - her still clutching the goldfish.

As the guests arrived and took their seats, I was given the nod to start my solo set. The rest of the band sat outside in the sun, pulling faces at me through the huge great patio door I swapped spots with our guitarist, who won the audience over for a few songs before the speeches and related formalities started.

While the speeches were taking place, we did our best to keep out of the way. However, we failed dismally with our giggling about the goldfish (amongst other things) and garnered several filthy looks from the bride's mother. We had been suitably Paddington-stare reprimanded and shuffled off to sit quietly at the bar before we were due to go on in a few minutes.

Asking the barmaid for a glass of water each for the band seemed to be a mammoth request. She put 12 bottles of Perrier onto a large silver tray and opened each one of them slowly. Once they were all opened, she looked up at me,

'Fourteen pounds fifty, Luv,' she said as she reached out her hand. I only wanted tap water and didn't expect to be asked to pay for bottled water. It was an unbearably hot summer day, and there was no way we could play for two hours (two of us had already played an hour each) without some water. Besides, I'd kind of assumed that we wouldn't have to pay for it.

I told the barmaid that the waters were 'for the bride.' I've learned over the years that this is the International Answer to any seemingly unreasonable request at a wedding. She seemed okay with that and let us take them.

OK, so we're a tribute band. We play Madness songs. Only Madness songs. Is that easy enough to understand? Apparently not. As the wedding party got drunker, the less they could comprehend this reasonably simple piece of information.

'Play some Bryan Adams' was called out more times than I cared to remember.

'WHY WON'T YOU PLAY SUMMER OF 69?'

'Oh, go on... just once, do you know it? It goes, 'I got ma first real sick thing, poured it on the five oh nine.'

Shoot me now.

After packing away and getting paid, our guitarist sat by himself, staring into space with his wallet perched on his knee. I wandered over to see if he was ok. He and I had become close friends, and I thoroughly cherished his company, so I crouched down on the floor and asked what was wrong.

'I just got paid pretty handsomely for doing something I'd gladly do for nothing,' he said, holding his wallet up. His eyes were glassy, and he looked fit to burst into tears.

'This weekend I've earned more than I earn in a week sitting at my desk,' he continued shaking his head.

I don't know where it came from. It's a phrase I've never said before or since, but I smiled up at him,

'Stick with me, kid,' I grinned, putting on a frankly terrible American accent.

He did. Rob and I have been happily married for over ten years now.

My front left tyre hit something hard in the road on the way home from that gig at about 2 in the morning. Of course, you already know about the red-bearded-taxidermist-cum-pickup-truck-driver from the start of this adventure. Aside from the dead animal chatter, he helped me make it home without any other issues. We pulled up outside my house, and I profusely thanked my Knight in Shining Armour. His vast red beard was littered with bits of what I can only assume was his lunch, but his smile was genuine, and I'd enjoyed his company. He clearly loved his job, and it made me wonder if perhaps he took the driving job purely so that he could find stuff to stuff.

There were a couple of bits of paperwork to sign, and then we were left with just the tiny issue of the cash to be handed over for my renewed membership. I reached into my wallet and pulled out all the money I'd earned for the wedding gig. He didn't have any change, so technically, I'd spent the evening making nothing. At least I now knew how to skin a squirrel should I ever find the need to. I joked with my new bearded friend about my predicament.

'Sarah, I have to ask...' he said in earnest, putting his hand on my arm as I got out of the truck,

'Why do you keep playing such shitty gigs? Surely there must be something better out there.'

Aside from his suggestion to write a book about my adventures, this was the other life-changing glass-shattering d'oh-why-didn't-I-think-of-that thing he said. It was like I'd been walloped in the face with a stuffed badger. How was this unassuming amateur taxidermist so damned astute?

I fulfilled the remainder of my pub gig agreements and never booked another one again. Then I began seeking out session work, attentive audiences, and exclusively ticketed shows. Rob and I formed a duo and started writing original material. We're currently working on our 8th album. Almost every story in this book is from before we started working together. Back when I exclusively played shit gigs. People often ask me for advice on how to stop playing shit gigs. It's simple. Stop booking shit gigs.

I can confidently say now that I make a comfortable living as a not-remotely-well-known musician. I still have the occasional gig-from-hell, but not so many, thanks to a man who picked up broken cars for a living and broken carcasses for a hobby.

Authors note

I can't thank you enough for buying this book and, more importantly, making it to the end!

I wrote this at a time when I truly believed I'd never be physically able to get on stage again after complications with partial bilateral lung collapse due to COVID-19 complications. I'm thrilled to say that I am back to full health (touch wood) and we're currently planning our busiest year of touring yet. Looking back on these gigs has made me realise how far in my distant memory they thankfully are.

I am utterly amazed that, despite almost every gig in the early days being a soul-destroying shit-show, I persevered with it. The drive and passion in a musician - in any creative person - cannot be quelled. If I've scared you off with my tales of penny-pinching and bad promoter bingo, be assured - it will get better. But only if you work at it. ALL. THE. TIME. No one cares about your career as much as you do.

Gigantinormous thanks to my husband Rob. Without you, I simply wouldn't be where I am today in any aspect of my life. Your support, your companionship, your wicked sense of humour and your musicianship make you sparkle and I am bewildered but grateful daily why you chose such a mental ginger bird to be your wife. You're my rock.

Thank you also to my son, Charlie. An inspiration, a dear friend and a world-class creative genius. A man who succeeds beyond belief at whatever he turns his hand to. You rock, Charlington Bilberry McFlumpletTrumpet III.

Thank you so much to my beta readers, especially John Tuck and Tanya Speight who read through my drafts of this book with a fine tooth comb. Any spelling or grammatical errors you may have found here are entirely deliberate and intended as further proof (should you require any) of my quirkiness.

And last, but by no means least, to you dear reader. Whether you're already a fan of our music or whether you stumbled across this book and thought you'd give it a shot, you've made my day. Why don't you drop me a line? (info@reddirtskinners.com)

If you fancy checking out our music or coming to a show, you can find us at www.reddirtskinners.com I promise I never swear on stage just in case you're worried about bringing your gran to a show.

If you fancy leaving a review, please head on over to Amazon right now. Even if it's just a one-sentence comment, it'll make a huge difference. This book is funded by fan support and is self-published. Reviews are a huge boost to independent creatives like us who don't have support from big publishing names or labels. The more reviews, the more people might find this book, and that helps put food on the table. And we like food.

43856003R00120